Praise for *Chocolate & Vicodin*

"In search of relief from the headache that wouldn't go away, Jennette Fulda shares her grueling journey through the mad, mad world of modern, managed-care medicine. Smart, unflinchingly honest, and laugh-out-loud funny, *Chocolate & Vicodin* kept me turning the pages, hoping to find her cure on the next one, or maybe the next one."

—Lisa Genova, *New York Times* bestselling author of *Still Alice* and *Left Neglected*

"This book is sharply observed, weirdly suspenseful, and refreshingly honest. Jennette Fulda helps to bring the long-misunderstood and inherently absurd illness of chronic daily headache out of the closet, exposing the devastation it wreaks on every part of one's life—and she's really, really funny in the process. But you don't have to be battling an epic headache or other wily chronic illness to appreciate it; I also recommend the book to anyone who just enjoys being in the intimate company of a talented storyteller with a strong, original voice."

—Paula Kamen, author of *All in My Head: An Epic Quest to Cure an Unrelenting, Totally Unreasonable, and Only Slightly Enlightening Headache*

"*Chocolate & Vicodin* will resonate deeply with anyone blindsided by pain. Using her trademark humor and grit, blogger and author Jennette Fulda unmasks invisible disease with equal parts insight and skepticism. As she wades through doctor treatments, tests, and the steady flow of comments from the blogosphere, Fulda's memoir emerges as more than a quest for healing but a hard-fought journey to reclaim her identity, a triumph so many readers facing chronic pain will appreciate."

—Laurie Edwards, author of *Life Disrupted: Getting Real About Chronic Illness in Your Twenties and Thirties*

Praise for *Half-Assed*

"A winsome, charming memoir of personal discovery."

—*Kirkus Reviews*

"Touching, funny, and sincere."

—*Shape*

***Chocolate & Vicodin* is also available as an eBook.**

CHOCOLATE & VICODIN

My Quest for Relief from the Headache That Wouldn't Go Away

Jennette Fulda

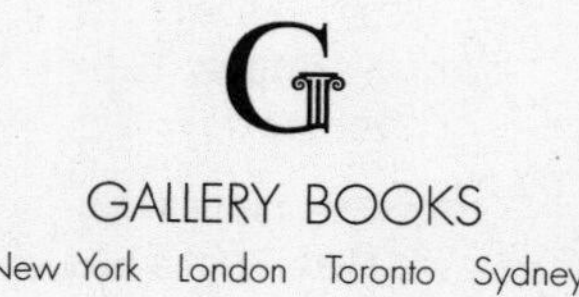

GALLERY BOOKS
New York London Toronto Sydney

Gallery Books
A Division of Simon & Schuster, Inc.
1230 Avenue of the Americas
New York, NY 10020

First Gallery Books trade paperback edition February 2011

GALLERY BOOKS and colophon are trademarks of Simon & Schuster, Inc.

For information about special discounts for bulk purchases, please contact Simon & Schuster Special Sales at 1-866-506-1949 or business@simonandschuster.com.

The Simon & Schuster Speakers Bureau can bring authors to your live event. For more information or to book an event, contact the Simon & Schuster Speakers Bureau at 1-866-248-3049 or visit our website at www.simonspeakers.com.

Designed by Ruth Lee-Mui

Manufactured in the United States of America

1 3 5 7 9 10 8 6 4 2

Library of Congress Cataloging-in-Publication Data

Fulda, Jennette.
Chocolate & Vicodin : my quest for relief from the headache that wouldn't go away / By Jennette Fulda.
p. cm.
1. Fulda, Jennette—Health. 2. Headache—Patients—United States—Biography. I. Title.
RC392.F85 2011
362.196'84910092—dc22
2010041735

ISBN 978-1-4391-8202-4
ISBN 978-1-4391-8209-3 (ebook)

For all those who suffer.

(This book works better than a placebo. I swear.)

Author's Note

All the events in this book happened (unfortunately), but the timeline has been adjusted slightly to accommodate the story arc. I have changed the names of most characters and altered the physical descriptions of people and places to make them unidentifiable. A few characters are composites of multiple people. All emails included in the text were really sent to me (and are reproduced here as written). No, you may not have my email address.

1

The Headache

It would be easier if I'd been hit by a truck. Then I would have a story for how it began. I could start with how I jogged into the intersection after the "Walk" sign had lit up. The cherry-red pickup truck would slam me in the sternum and punt me across the street. Then both the ambulance siren and I would scream on the way to the hospital, where doctors with unfamiliar faces would save my life.

But I wasn't hit by a truck, or even a Volkswagen Bug. I was hit by a headache. Just like many victims of car accidents, I can't remember the moment of impact. I'll never know if the pain arrived before lunch, after dinner, or while I was in the shower. All I know is that sometime on February 17, 2008, the headache greeted me by hugging my skull tightly, like a grandparent I hadn't seen for years, and wouldn't let go.

I didn't deem its arrival worth remembering because it was an ordinary tension headache, the kind that sells millions of over-the-counter pain relievers a year. The only remarkable thing was that it wouldn't go away. The pain manifested itself as pressure in my forehead, nose, and sinuses, as if I had encountered a poltergeist that preferred to press down on my face rather than rearrange my living room furniture.

I do remember that I became concerned on the third day. The only things that should take three days are resurrections, not headaches. For the first few days, I'd tried to exorcise my painful ghost with pills. I took Tylenol and then Advil and then aspirin and then Aleve, showing no brand loyalty in my choice of painkillers. Nothing worked.

On the morning of the third day, I plodded barefoot into the kitchen of my one-bedroom apartment to make breakfast. I paused and looked at the sink, and then slowly took two more steps toward the stainless-steel basin. There were black dots forming on my dirty soup bowl. Was that . . . mold? I hadn't had the energy to lift a scrub pad since the headache arrived. Instead I'd spent the previous night lying on the love seat with my head on the pillows, watching a marathon of *House,* a TV show about patients with strange diseases. I was now concerned that I might be dying of lupus *and* a tropical brain virus. I also wanted Dr. House to give me his Vicodin.

Now that I thought about it, when was the last time I'd flossed? Made my bed? Exercised? For the past three days, I'd barely managed to drag my body to work and back home. There had been no time for chores. My world was limited to the size of my skull, which ached incessantly as though my brain had a muscle cramp. How could my life fall apart in three days? If I actually had been hit by a truck, I'd have an understandable excuse. Being run over by a headache seemed ridiculous. I should be able to take an Excedrin and just get over it. What would hit me next? A fatal case of athlete's foot?

This wasn't my first encounter with a lingering headache. Six years ago, I'd gotten one that lasted an entire month. I'd gone to the doctor, who gave me a small blue-and-white capsule to take every night. This beta-blocker had kicked the headache out of my head and out of my mind, too. Since then I'd basically forgotten I'd had a problem with headaches. My only reminder was the pill I still took every night, which was now suddenly useless.

The reappearance of this problem was particularly stunning because I was literally in the best health of my life. I'd lost almost two hundred pounds over the past few years by dieting and exercising. Everyone was so amazed by my accomplishment that I was amazed by myself, too. I felt like the astounding weight-loss girl, who could tackle any obstacle and achieve any goal. I had life completely figured out.

For my next impossible feat, I was running a half-marathon in May, partly as a media stunt for the release of a memoir I'd written about my weight loss. I was excited about the book's upcoming publication, like an expectant mother waiting for her due date. So I was concerned that I hadn't exercised this week. I didn't want to gain weight right before the book release, and if I didn't continue training for my half-marathon I'd never be in good enough shape to complete it. I wasn't going to get across the finish line with fuzzy teeth and moldy soup bowls. The headache needed to go away because I had not invited it to my book release party.

I called the doctor later that morning, right after I arrived at my typical office with its typical cubicles and typical monotony. As I listened to the phone ring, I had plenty of time to stare at an atypical water stain on the ceiling tile and wonder if toxic mold was triggering my pain. Later that day I sat in a sterile, white examination room, crinkling the white tissue paper covering the table, letting my feet dangle slightly off the floor.

I had come to the doctor as a matter of course, just as I would have gone to the mechanic if I were having problems with my car. The doctor would give me a new pill that would fix me, just as the mechanic would change my oil filter, and that would be that, I was sure. This was how the world worked.

"So, your headache is acting up again?" Dr. Rodgers half asked, half stated, from her perch on a black swiveling stool. Her amber eyes were scanning my chart. I watched them dart back and forth beneath her wire-frame glasses. "Do you still take Inderal LA?" she asked.

"Yep, every night for six years now. I've been fine until last Sunday."

The doctor looked up from her notes and asked me, "Has anything changed in your life recently that might have triggered this?"

"I did just start a new job," I told her. I had been a web designer for a local media company in Indianapolis for a little more than a month now. I had worked for a small design firm for four years after college, but then took my latest position because it paid better and provided health insurance. Actually, it would provide health insurance after I'd worked there for three months—which was still two months away. This was a detail that seemed a lot more pertinent now than it had been when I was hired. I was still covered by the insurance from a contracting job I'd done in the interim, but the coverage wasn't very comprehensive.

"Is the new job stressful?" the doctor asked.

"Not terribly so," I replied. "I'm still catching up, which is a bit stressful, but the people have been really nice." I felt proud about my new web design job. My co-workers were all smart and good at what they did, and working with them confirmed my own belief that I was smart and good at what I did, too.

Dr. Rodgers finished taking my history and closed my chart. "We'll try giving you a shot first, which will hopefully abort the headache. If that doesn't work, we'll try upping your dosage of Inderal," she said as she wrote a prescription. "Your symptoms might just be the flu. However, I'll also give you a free sample of Imitrex to try, which helps with migraines."

"Migraines? Do I really have a migraine?" I didn't know what officially qualified a headache as a migraine, but I'd heard they were like ice cream headaches without the benefit of the ice cream. I didn't have a distinct, stabbing pain like that. I had an indistinct yet agonizing feeling of tension and pressure.

"Migraines don't always present with the same symptoms for

everyone. I'm not sure if your headache is a migraine, but it won't hurt to try the Imitrex."

Dr. Rodgers left, and the round-cheeked nurse with smiling eyes came in to shoot Toradol into my thigh. "This usually aborts a headache," she said as she filled a syringe with medication. "It's an NSAID, a nonsteroidal anti-inflammatory drug."

"Oh, okay," I said, as if I understood what that meant. I looked at the needle as though she were holding a small crocodile.

The nurse saw my expression. "Don't worry. If I stick it in fast you'll barely feel it. It's only if you slowly insert the needle that it's painful. So it's better if I jab you with it." I tried to believe what she was saying, then turned my head away to focus my gaze on the suddenly fascinating venetian blinds. I felt a prick, like a mean third-grader pinching my leg.

"All done."

I drove home happy to know that my headache would soon be gone. I lay down on my love seat, which was too small for my whole body. My knees were left elevated on the plush arm, and my toes dangled off the end as they had when I sat on the doctor's table.

I lived alone, except for my two cats, Java Bean and Officer Krupke. I had a cute one-bedroom apartment near a somewhat trendy part of Indianapolis called Broad Ripple. I liked living near boutiques, restaurants, and the nature trail, but my previous salary had made it impossible for me to afford spending any money in this neighborhood.

I'd been optimistic lately because I had a new, better-paying job and my book was coming out soon. Since I'd started losing weight three years ago, life had only been getting better, month after month. I'd been going out more, my writing career held promise, and I was more confident than I'd ever been. I felt that I was part of the world now, instead of watching it pass me by. This medical setback was inconceivable. Now I knew what it must feel like to be a stock trader blindsided by a market crash.

I continued to lie on my love seat, staring at my stuffed monkey doll, which dangled from a hook in the ceiling, waiting for the medication to kick in. Three hours later I was still waiting.

Was it possible to get a refund for drugs that didn't work?

I took the Imitrex that night, part of the sample pill pack the doctor had given me. It was a migraine abortive to be taken when a migraine was coming on, which meant I was swallowing it three days too late. But the doctor had given me a pill, so I took it. I went to bed hoping I'd wake up to discover the headache had been just a bad dream.

The unicorn in the cabinet was angry that we had left him crackers instead of Oreos and was going to report me to my boss, but before I could tell him the grocery store had rejected my credit card, the fire alarm started wailing, BUZZ, BUZZ, BUZZ, and I opened my eyes to smack my alarm clock and momentarily forgot that my head hurt. That moment didn't last long.

The only thing worse than the pain was the fact that I couldn't think about anything but the pain. The headache was like a crush that was always on my mind, and it felt like it was crushing my mind, too. As I'd lain in bed the night before, I'd thought only of the headache caressing my skull with its porcupine skin. As I drove to work, I considered nothing but the headache's single-minded devotion to me. As I stared at my computer monitor, the headache made my nerves buzz and tingle. I'd scheduled a follow-up appointment with Dr. Rodgers, but it was still days away. Until then, I was doomed to repeat my miserable routine.

"I hope it's not a brain tumor," I said aloud to my co-worker Sarah, solely so she would reassure me that it wasn't a brain tumor.

"It's not a brain tumor," Sarah replied, fulfilling her role diligently. We sat at a white laminate lunch table in the office cafeteria. Sarah was my leading contender for the available position of "Best Friend from Work." She was eating soup, and I was chewing on stale candy hearts, though I wasn't sure if candy hearts ever really went stale.

"It might be something in the air system, like Legionnaires' disease. Does anyone else have a headache?" I asked her.

"Not that I know of," she replied, pushing a stray brown curl behind her ear. "Besides, you've only been here a month. Everyone else has been here longer and they're not sick."

It was true. Damn Sarah, the computer programmer, and her unassailable logic. "This is weird, though. Why won't my stupid headache go away?"

"I don't know," she said. Her brown eyes expressed sympathy. "Don't worry. Headaches don't last forever," she told me. Then she slurped her soup.

"I know. It will probably go away soon. I'm just being a hypochondriac."

When we returned to our desks, I started posing my questions to the Internet instead of to my co-workers. I discovered there were eleventy-billion reasons a human being could have a headache, but all I could focus on were the words "brain tumor."

It had to be cancer. I always assumed it was cancer. Any ache or pain was probably the first sign of a tumor that was going to slowly and painfully kill me as I lay on my deathbed wondering why I'd ignored the early warning signs. After all the worrying I had done about cancer, I was going to be seriously disappointed if I did not one day die of a tumor.

Dr. Google returned a list of brain tumor symptoms for me, the first of which made me hold my breath in fear:

- Headaches that gradually become more frequent and more severe

As I read the rest of the symptoms, I began to breathe again:

- Unexplained nausea or vomiting
- Vision problems, such as blurred vision, double vision, or loss of peripheral vision
- Gradual loss of sensation or movement in an arm or a leg
- Difficulty with balance
- Speech difficulties
- Confusion in everyday matters
- Personality or behavior changes
- Seizures, especially in someone who doesn't have a history of seizures
- Hearing problems

Well, I didn't have any of that, except for the headache part, and the entry said only a small number of headache sufferers had brain tumors. I checked other medical web sites, and they all agreed. I didn't have a tumor.

However, I *did* have an active imagination and an active Internet connection. I pulled out a notebook from my desk drawer and scrawled down my theories as if I were the star of *Nancy Drew and the Case of the Mysterious Headache*. I'd recently begun drinking coffee, so perhaps I was getting too much caffeine. Alas, the Internet said caffeine alleviated headaches in the proper dosage. I typed in "seasonal affective disorder" because I'd been feeling tired lately and hoped the cure would be a mandatory Caribbean cruise, but headaches weren't listed as a symptom. I considered searching for "allergies," but my younger brother was the one who'd had to get allergy shots, not me. After more searching, sinusitis came up and after reading about the disease, I was sure I'd found a winner. I decided to ignore the fact that if you took out the three *s*'s and *i*'s in "sinusitis," you were left with the word "nut."

A few days later my feet were dangling above the floor at the doctor's office again.

"How are you doing?" Dr. Rodgers asked, and I was puzzled. When people asked you how you were doing, they didn't really want to know how you were doing. They were saying, "I am a human and you are a human and we are passing in the hallway, so I'll acknowledge your existence and inquire about your mood to avoid awkwardly staring at the walls, but I don't care how you actually feel."

I didn't know how to respond in this case. I was obviously here for the second time this week because I did not feel well, yet the words "Oh, okay" stumbled out of my mouth robotically.

"You still have your headache?" she asked, sounding surprised as she read the nurse's report. I momentarily hated her for going home, watching TV, and sleeping in her bed without having to think about my pain. I didn't have the luxury of forgetting it for even a commercial break.

"Yeah, it just won't go away. The shot you gave me didn't help at all." I shifted uncomfortably, though not because of the chair. "Actually, I think it might be my sinuses. Could it be a bacterial infection? You know, sinusitis?" I shouldn't have to say this. She was the doctor. She was supposed to be smarter than me. If I actually had sinusitis, she should have figured it out already. I was going to make her look stupid if I was right. Or I would look stupid if I was wrong. But I thought it was sinusitis. I wanted it to be sinusitis. It had to be sinusitis! I wanted to slap a name on this problem, define its edges, and make it something known rather than claw against a disease without a title I could curse. Pain was a sign that something was wrong, and sinusitis was as good a disease to blame as any.

She prescribed antibiotics and gave me samples of an antihistamine and decongestant in case it was allergies. Then she wrote an order for a sinus CT scan to be done if I wasn't feeling better in a week. I sped away to the nearest pharmacy. It was closed. I drove to the second-closest pharmacy and waited in a stiffly padded chair as the woman in a white coat filled my prescription.

It had been a week now. Seven days. 168 hours. 10,080 minutes. 604,800 seconds of pain. Constant pain. It gnawed on my nerves with formless teeth as I sipped my coffee. It flicked at my synapses as I sat at the computer clicking the mouse. It tap danced across my forehead out of time to the music playing in my earphones. Worst of all, it was a shiny object distracting my attention, a small child screaming, "Look at me! Look at me! Are you looking at me?!" There was no room for thoughts about plans for the weekend and what to eat for dinner. The headache was all there was now. It had started in my forehead and extended its tendrils outward until it encompassed my whole life. I was the headache and the headache was me.

But now the nice lady in the white jacket was handing me the magic pills and I would become myself again. I rushed to the car and pushed the first pill of the five-day treatment out of its foil packet. I swallowed it dry.

Five days later I was still the headache and the headache was still me.

I was horribly disappointed. I'd really been hoping for a bacterial infection.

I dialed the phone number to schedule a CT scan. "We've got a spot available in one week," the receptionist told us.

"One week?" I croaked. "Isn't there anything sooner?"

"Sorry," she replied.

The headache giggled at me. We had at least seven more days together. It had another week to squat in my brain uninvited. I had to wait today and tomorrow and the day after that and after that for no real reason. I had to suffer all of this waiting, just to have a test that might or might not reveal the cause of my problem. I wanted to do something, anything. I needed to get better, and I needed to do it now.

I would approach this practically, in an organized, non-hysterical manner because that was how I'd attacked my weight problem, too. There was no reason to get emotional. I would make a plan and execute it and then I would get better. I had googled the right terms and I had seen my doctor and now I would try more over-the-counter medication.

I wandered into the pharmacy aisle at my drugstore to gaze at the wall of medications. There were decongestants, antihistamines, nonsteroidal anti-inflammatory drugs, nasal sprays, painkillers, vitamins, minerals, and more. They came in pills and gel caps and candy-coated capsules. They were sold under both generic and name brands.

The contents of one of these containers would ease my pain. I knew this intuitively. It had to be true because the alternative was unthinkable. I needed to get better. It had been almost two weeks. I just had a headache. Everybody gets headaches. They take pills and they get better. Twenty-seven-year-old women did not sleepwalk through their lives in constant pain.

This was a game now. I would keep trying new pills and hope I didn't run out of room in my medicine cabinet. I read the active ingredients. I read the symptoms the pills would cure. I spent fifteen minutes in the medicine aisle. I went to the counter to buy the stuff they couldn't sell me without ID because I might make meth out of it. I took everything home and tried the medications, one at a time, day after day after day.

I was still the headache and the headache was still me.

As I waited for the date of my CT scan, there was plenty of time for the headache and me to look through our memories together. Had something changed that I had overlooked? Was I somehow to blame? The memories flashed past me like a slide show at hyper-speed. There were so many variables. The job, my diet, the weather. Anything tangible or intangible became suspect.

I flipped back further through my memories, and stopped on a scene from when I was seven years old. Memories of my childhood were sometimes cloudy and hard to read, like an ancient hard drive struggling to spin, but this one was particularly vivid.

I am playing with Carrie Atwater on the elementary school playground. Carrie is sitting down at the top of the slide and rubbing her head.

"What's wrong?" I ask from where I stand on the ladder behind her.

"I have a headache," she says.

"What's a headache feel like?" I ask. I've never had a headache and I am jealous. Carrie Atwater has a fluffy black poodle, a Nintendo, and a Barbie dream house. I have none of these things, and now Carrie Atwater has a headache, too. I want a headache!

"It just hurts," she says and then pushes off down the slide.

I continued to flip through my memories and stopped on a scene that played out when I was thirteen.

I am watching TV with my friend Kathy in her living room. We're singing the lyrics to "A Whole New World" while watching Aladdin. *She is singing Jasmine's part and I am singing Aladdin's part. Kathy stops singing and leans forward on the couch, moaning and clasping her arms around her belly. "Are you okay?" I ask, excited that I might get to call 911 or perform CPR, like I learned in health class.*

"Yeah, I'm fine. It's just menstrual cramps," she replies. I nod as if I understand, but I don't because I'd never had menstrual cramps. I still haven't gotten my period. I want my period and I want cramps because everyone else has them and I don't.

I sighed in self-admonishment. One day I would finally get cramps and I would finally get a headache, but as soon as I got these things I would only want to give them back.

I sped forward through my slide show of memories and stopped to focus on a single picture. *Remember this?* the headache asked. I did remember this. I liked to pretend it had never happened, burying it under a pile of pills, each one taken once at bedtime. The memory was six years old, speckled with dust. *This was when we first met.*

I am twenty-one and I'm driving down State Road 31 in my cobalt-blue Honda Civic. I am traveling from Indianapolis to visit a friend in South Bend, a three-hour trip if you drive like I do. The traffic slows, and I see roadblocks past the Arby's and a state trooper standing guard. Confused, I pull up to the trooper, who tells me there has been a chemical spill on the highway and I must take a detour.

I follow the other cars like lemmings headed off a cliff (if there were cliffs in rural Indiana). I pull off the road and look at the map my mother insisted I take along and try to determine where to stick the "You are here" sign. I drive in the other direction and go through a stop sign, turn around and go through the stop sign again, then turn around until I've gone all four possible ways through the stop sign, finally certain I am headed in the right direction. I find the highway without first running out of gas, relieved because I don't own a cell phone yet.

I am speeding down the highway, stressed out because I was lost and I am now late. My head starts to hurt and the muscles in my neck clench tightly like a baby's fist. I whiz through the stoplight and there are flashing lights in the side mirror. I pull over and clumsily drop the name of my friend who works as a clerk in the local police department. He is state police and doesn't care, but I get off with a warning anyway. The warning is that my head is going to implode.

I reach my friend's house and sit on the couch watching the news report about the chemical spill. My head still hurts. It hurts all weekend and when I get home. It hurts at my job designing business cards and fliers. It hurts for a month before I finally go to the doctor with the wire-frame glasses and amber eyes. She prescribes magic pills that chase the headache away.

I take the pills every night for years. Twice I try to go off them. This is a very bad, no-good, horrible idea. I bang my head on the pew in front of me at midnight mass. My Christmas gift to myself is a blue-and-white capsule.

I take the pills. The headache stays away. These are the rules.

The rules had changed.

2

Testing, 1, 2, Bleed

I had a blog called PastaQueen.com where I'd documented my weight loss and where I'd started documenting my headache. As any blogger knows, readers are more than happy to tell you what is wrong with you. Mine were no exception.

To: Jennette.Fulda@home

From: Deirdre@McDreamy

Subject: Possible headache diagnosis

Ok, this is gonna sound really frickin' stupid. And if you decide my suggestion is worthy of your shit list, so be it. I'll still enjoy your blog :)

Do you watch *Grey's Anatomy*? Ok, there was this one episode where the guy came in there with the headache that would not stop. He said it was a constant 8 out of 10. That they'd tried everything!!!!! But then that one intern remembered something about a rare condition caused by pressure on the anterior ethmoid nerve in the nose. I think it's called anterior ethmoid nerve syndrome . . . anyway, I think they did some quick test sticking something up his nose and that was it (hey, it was TV) . . . they took out his turbinate and he was fine. There are legitimate articles online about it..

I'm sorry if you hate me for offering up a suggestion. I just hate the thought of someone suffering constantly . . .

Well, either way, I hope your headache problem is solved soon.

Good luck,
Deirdre

I was now receiving dozens of emails listing possible causes and cures for my pain. Headaches are incredibly common, so there appeared to be hundreds, if not thousands, of possible reasons for my problem. I filed the emails away for potential use in the future but decided to go ahead with the CT scan recommended by a medical professional before turning to the advice of well-meaning Internet people.

One week after lying on a white table that swooped in and out of a large radioactive hula hoop, I was told I had beautiful sinuses. I wanted ugly ones. "So, um, what do we do next?" I asked the nurse who'd called me with my results. Soon my feet were dangling off the table at the doctor's office again. I always seemed to end up back here. My life kept going in circles.

"I'm going to order some blood tests. If those come back clean we'll send you for an MRI," Dr. Rodgers told me as she scrawled the lab orders. I grudgingly took the lab orders and wondered how many more days of pain I'd have to live through before my latest task was completed.

The next morning, my stomach was growling as I walked up and down the block in search of a medical lab. I'd fasted for twelve hours before my blood test, so the sight of the new Dunkin' Donuts on the corner had prompted a gastrointestinal symphony. I pulled out the folded piece of paper from my pocket to look at the address one more time, and finally realized my error. The location I'd looked up in the insurance provider booklet was on Pennsylvania *Street*, not Pennsylvania *Avenue*. I was nine miles south of where I was supposed to be.

I looked longingly through the store's windows and paused to inhale the smell of chocolate frosting and flour. Then I walked back to my car and drove to a nearby hospital that I knew for certain was on my insurance plan. I pressed my right index finger against my temple as I drove, unsuccessfully trying to ease the tension in my skull. I drove one-handed around the parking garage, circling a half-dozen times looking for a spot. Then I looped up and down the hallways of the hospital before finally finding the lobby of the lab.

"Hi," I greeted the receptionist. "Is this the place where I can have my blood drawn?"

From behind the counter, a heavyset woman with a pale complexion raised an eyebrow at me, as though I'd just accused her of being a vampire. I handed her my lab orders, and she coolly told me to sit down and wait until someone was available to process me.

I turned around and walked slowly through the waiting room, strategically assessing the seating situation. The place was packed, probably with other fasters hungry for breakfast like me. I eliminated any seats directly next to another person, leaving me with three options. Two seats were conveniently pointed toward the TV set, but only one was also next to a table with magazines. That was the seat I collapsed in.

The cushy, vinyl chairs in the waiting room looked like they'd been bought in the seventies. The orange and olive colors reminded me of my mother's cookware. I preferred my primary care physician's waiting room, which had newer chairs and a flat-screen TV, unlike the bulky cathode ray television here.

I tried to read a *Time* magazine, but the headache scratched against the back of my eyes like sandpaper, making the sentences seem like strings of random words shoved together. My hunger made me restless, anyway. I looked around the waiting room and saw a man and a woman with greasy hair. A teenage boy sat in a chair to my right, nestled in an oversize coat bearing a Colts logo. He must have been missing school to be here, but I wondered if he'd have preferred to be in math class. I assessed the rest of my silent comrades. They were black, white, Hispanic, and Indian. Some were slumped back impatiently, while others fidgeted nervously. One was missing several teeth. I couldn't imagine all of us meeting together anywhere else. The only thing we had in common was that none of us wanted to be here. Illness was the great equalizer. It didn't care if you had teeth.

"Janet Fulda?" The woman from the front desk was now standing with a clipboard in her hand as she called out a mispronunciation of my name. This happened a lot at Starbucks, too, but at least there I could get something to eat.

"Jennette. That's me," I told her. I followed her back to a desk made of cheap laminated wood that was peeling at the edges. I sat down opposite her, and she began typing information into a computer.

"You ever been a patient here before?" she asked, her eyes still fixed on the monitor.

"Nope." I gave her my social security number and enough personal information to ruin me.

"Looks like we have a Joyce Fulda in the system. Your address the same as hers?"

"Oh, that's my mom." That reminded me that I needed to call my mother about my normal CT results. She lived in town, and I'd told her about my headache problem last week during one of our frequent phone calls. She was worried about my headache, as any mother would be. "No. We have different addresses. I'm surprised she's in there. I can't remember her coming here, at least not since I was born."

The woman made eye contact with me for the first time since we'd sat down. "You were born here?" she asked.

"Yeah."

She arched her perfectly plucked eyebrow and pinned me with an accusing glare. "So you *have* been a patient here before." Did she expect me to apologize for not remembering being born? Or was it standard procedure to roil a patient's blood before drawing it?

After the woman entered my information into the system, I happily left her presence and returned to the waiting room. Twenty minutes later I was well-acquainted with the news loop on the twenty-four-hour news channel. I checked my watch as I had done every minute since I'd been here and recalculated how late I was going to be to work. A tall man in blue scrubs walked into the waiting room, and I stared at him expectantly. He'd called several names, none of which were mine, until now.

"Janet Fulda?" he asked the room.

"That's me," I replied, so happy to leave that I didn't bother to correct him. I dropped the issue of *Time* I wasn't reading on the table and walked back through a hallway with him as he hummed.

"So what are we testing you for?" he asked as he scanned my sheet. *Doobley-boopty-doo,* he sang to himself.

"I . . . have a headache," I told him. *Boo-dop-ba-dum,* he hummed as he led me to a stall. I sat down in a chair that had a high, cushioned armrest and watched him arrange a sterilized packet of tools on a tray. The room smelled like plastic and Band-Aids.

"Is one arm better than the other for you?" he asked.

"I have absolutely no idea," I told him. The last time I'd had blood drawn was four years earlier during a gallbladder attack, and all I remembered was almost passing out. Not even a free cookie could entice me to donate blood voluntarily.

He tied an elastic band around my arm, which had made me feel light-headed four years ago, but at the present moment all I could focus on was his humming. I considered offering to buy him a radio if he would stop but decided not to antagonize the man with the needle. I looked away, toward the sterile white curtain dividing my stall from the next, as he stuck the needle into my arm.

"Whoops, didn't make it," he said. *Doo-doo-waddly-doo.* "Your veins roll. They're pretty small too."

"I'm sorry?" If I could have made my veins the size of garden hoses, I would have done it just to get out of there. The humming phlebotomist stuck me again, and this time I started to bleed properly into the plastic tubing. He filled three vials, taped a cotton pad onto my arm with hot-pink medical tape, and I finally escaped the building.

After handing a five-dollar bill to the parking garage operator, I sped into the street toward my office, thinking only of the two packets of oatmeal waiting in the top left drawer of my desk. My head was throbbing intensely now. Was it possible that the stress, exhaustion, and hunger had caused me to have a regular headache on top of my chronic headache? I wanted to bang my head on the steering wheel in time with the throbbing or crawl into the backseat to nap. Instead, I turned left down the street that ran past my office building.

That was when I saw six pairs of headlights speeding toward me.

I was suddenly very much awake as I realized I had not turned onto the street that ran past my office building. I was one block off and heading the wrong way down a one-way street. A bearded man in a red Toyota Corolla honked loudly as he slowed down to prevent a head-on collision. I could not hear what he was saying as I watched his lips move, but I did not think he was telling me how lovely my naturally curly hair looked that morning. I quickly shifted into reverse, threw my arm over the back of the passenger's seat, and drove down Michigan Street backward. Once I passed the intersection, I shifted into drive and turned right onto the street perpendicular to me, now headed in the correct direction.

I walked into the office at 10:04 A.M., more than an hour late. I dropped my purse on my desk, opened the top drawer, took out two oatmeal packets, and headed for the kitchen to drown my misery in a bowl of cinnamon swirl oatmeal.

It had only taken fifteen seconds for my doctor to write the lab order, yet it had taken me a long morning filled with hunger, the sound of insufferable humming, and a near car crash to complete the task she'd given me. Being sick was time-consuming work, and it was work that was twice as hard to complete when you were ill. I was lucky that I could come in late to work as long as I stayed late, too. Some people would have been fired from their jobs for being tardy. And it was frustrating that I wasn't guaranteed the blood test would give me any answers. I could have died in traffic today for nothing.

I had been awake for only three hours, but I was ready for the day to be over. I was ready for every day like this to be over.

• • •

I checked my voice mail three days later to hear the friendly voice of the nurse going on about how damn healthy I was. The blood panel had come back normal. I'd have to get an MRI.

This was a problem.

I'd worked at my job for a little over two months now, but my new health insurance didn't start until the first day of the month after three months of employment. That was three weeks and five days away. In the meantime, I was covered by the somewhat crappy insurance plan offered by the contracting agency I had previously worked for. I had scanned my insurance handbook and seen that they only covered up to $2,000 of medical testing a year. I'd already used part of that for my CT scan. How much did an MRI cost?

I sat in my car during my lunch break to covertly call local hospitals. I had no privacy in my cubicle, and I didn't want my boss discovering that his new employee was broken. Instead, I would risk having him think I was secretly interviewing for other jobs. Navigating the complicated rules and regulations of health insurance policies gave normal people headaches, so it was one of the last things I wanted to do while in constant pain. I could think of better ways to spend my lunch break, too, all of which involved eating lunch.

I was put on hold while I tried to find the answer to this simple question: How much does an MRI cost? Unbeknownst to me, this was like walking into a foreign marketplace and asking, "How much for that bracelet?" It cost what you would pay for it. I later learned that hospitals negotiate different rates with different insurance companies, so the same procedure can cost different amounts depending on your carrier. An insurance carrier with a large clientele can demand lower rates because the hospital can't survive without that company's business. I was a lone woman with a somewhat crappy insurance plan and little leverage. The customer service representative finally got back on the line with me and wouldn't give me an exact number but told me it could cost anywhere from $2,000 to $3,000.

Dragging an answer out of the customer service representative drained me of what little strength I had. I rubbed my temples and waited until the next day to call my insurance company. They confirmed that they wouldn't cover the procedure because it was over and above the amount covered in my policy. A friend of mine who'd survived cancer had told me that her hospital had written off a large amount of her $50,000 bill and negotiated a much smaller amount for her to pay. Sadly, I technically could afford the MRI since I had several thousand dollars in savings, so I doubted I could get the same sort of discount. It also seemed it might be worth a couple grand to avoid spending hours on the phone negotiating with the hospital billing department.

That night I looked at the wall calendar in my kitchen. It was twenty-six days until May, the day my new coverage would kick in, and coincidentally also the day my weight-loss memoir would be released. Waiting would save me at least two-thirds of the price of the MRI. I flipped back a few months and saw that I'd had the headache for six weeks. I'd survived for that long. There were so many other things I'd rather do with that money. I could pay off half my car loan. I could buy food for almost a year. I could surprise every member of my family with a Wii gaming system. It was painful to think of spending $2,000 on a test that took less time to complete than the SAT.

Surely I could wait a few more weeks to save a few grand, right? I resented the fact that I had been put in a situation like this. Why hadn't America fixed the health care system? Why couldn't I have been born in Canada? Yet, as mad as I was, there was no one person to focus my anger on, only abstract systems and bureaucracies in which no particular individual was responsible for the failure of the whole.

In the days after I made the decision to delay the MRI, my mind frequently flipped back to the matter, questioning whether this was the right call and wondering if my decision could be deadly. I distracted myself with a long list of possible causes and cures I could check out in the meantime. My blog readers had continued to pelt me with hailstones of advice. There were at least twenty people who'd told me twenty different things that they knew were undoubtedly the sole cause of my headache. I started working through the list. At least none of the cures people had suggested cost $2,000.

I cut artificial sweeteners out of my diet and suddenly hated food. I wanted to spit out the bland, plain yogurt I tried to eat. I couldn't swallow coffee without adding three spoonfuls of sugar, which negated the reason I'd started drinking coffee—it had almost no calories. It didn't matter much because I cut out coffee the next day in case excessive caffeine was causing the headache. Caffeine in small doses was supposed to help headaches, but too much could make them worse. I had no real justification for drinking six cans of Diet Dr. Pepper every day anyway. I weaned myself off the soda slowly so I wouldn't cause a withdrawal headache, but after several days, my head still felt like an overstuffed plush doll and I was so sleepy that my keyboard looked like a good pillow.

I fiddled with the placement of my monitors at work and at home to ensure that eyestrain was not causing my pain. I adjusted and readjusted my seat to achieve the perfect ergonomic position. I brought a desk lamp into my office to ensure I had enough light. None of it helped, and all the fidgeting at my desk made me look neurotic.

I still wanted to blame seasonal affective disorder, even if it wasn't known to cause headaches. So I bought a powerful sunlamp online and sat in front of it for twenty minutes each morning as I ate my oatmeal. I felt a little less sleepy in the mornings, though not enough to compensate for the lack of coffee. The headache wasn't vanquished by the light, but at least I was well armed against a vampire attack.

My mother had seen a neti pot used on *Oprah* and dropped one off at my apartment even though I'd told her my sinus CT was spectacular. A neti pot resembles a small plastic teapot, and it's used to treat hay fever or allergies. You're supposed to cram it up one nostril and tip your head sideways to send salt water through your nasal cavity and out the other nostril. I knew I'd look ridiculous, but by this point I was ready to run naked through the grocery store if doing so would cure me. The salt water made my nose burn and my eyes water, but the pain in my head remained.

I tracked my eating and kept a headache diary so I could

determine if a certain food was causing my headaches. The Internet revealed that common triggers were cheese, chocolate, and wine, though everyone could have their own unique triggers as well. I analyzed my diet and found absolutely no patterns. My headache went on without end, as seemingly infinite as the universe. If the headache were related to my diet, wouldn't it come and go, or at least flare up and die down, depending on what I ate?

Every day I ruminated on my situation for thirty minutes in the morning and thirty minutes in the evening when I commuted to and from work. Driving had become a dreaded task. It was complex enough to require part of my attention, yet not distracting enough for me to focus on something other than the pain in my head. It forced me to marinate in my migraine, and my mind always eventually turned to self-flagellation.

Could the headache be my own fault? I had spent many late nights staring at my computer screen last year when I was writing my book. Frequently I'd gone to bed with a headache that evaporated by the morning. Had all those little headaches taught my brain to be in pain so well that now it couldn't turn the feeling off? What about the LASIK surgery I'd had eighteen months ago? Could that have caused eyestrain? Or could the severing of nerves in my cornea have caused a chain reaction that led to the headache? What about my frequent jaw-clenching? Or that time I slipped on the ice at the beginning of January? Or the time the hairdresser singed my scalp with hot water? What if I hadn't taken this new job? What if something in my work environment had triggered the pain that could now never be turned off? Could the HPV vaccine I'd gotten last year have played a factor?

What if I had caught a virus that triggered all this? Would my whole situation be different if I'd just washed my hands more thoroughly?

Every time I slipped in my speech or garbled a word, I was worried that it was a warning sign of a tumor invading the language section of my brain. What if I really did have a tumor and delaying the MRI was going to cost me my life? But I didn't have a tumor. I knew I didn't. I didn't have the symptoms. I was always worried that I had cancer, but somehow I knew this headache wasn't a tumor. Unless it was. Which was more important, my health or the health of my bank account?

One Friday I was driving home from work, thinking about my headache as I always did, when I passed a theater marquee that said the band Stars was playing that night. I smiled quickly at the thought of one of my favorite bands and then consciously relaxed my face. Smiling hurt. So did laughing. I frequently pretended that my forehead had been Botoxed so I wouldn't flex the facial muscles that aggravated my headache.

I wanted to park my car on the street and buy a ticket to the concert, but I drove home to my apartment instead. The theater would be filled with cigarette smoke, which would make my head hurt even more. The headache was a chaperone preventing me from going out. There was no world outside the headache. There were no concerts or parties. My world was limited to the cubic dimensions of my skull.

I collapsed on my love seat and turned on the TV. I watched the local news, hoping to hear about someone whose life was worse than mine. The worst they could deliver were people upset about their property taxes. Next *24* came on, and I watched government super-agent Jack Bauer being tortured by terrorists. "Give it up, Jack. It's not worth it," I mumbled at the television. "Just tell them what they want to know." I would have given Osama bin Laden our nuclear launch codes by now, if only it would have made the pain go away.

My phone rang. I didn't answer it. I doubted I could focus on a conversation. There were fifteen more days until the first of May. I had assumed I would be spending April counting down the days until the release of my first book, but all I could think about was the MRI. I was never going to make it to May.

In grade school, we would sometimes make a game of asking friends what they would do for a million dollars. Would you eat someone else's snot? Would you walk to school naked? Would you French kiss your dog? It was fun to try to find something that wasn't worth a million dollars. Now I was playing the game for real, but the dollar amount had dropped. What would I do for $2,000? Could I spend two more weeks with the headache from hell?

If it had been a million dollars, I might have been able to hold out.

The headache had erected a wall between me and my former life. I had barely been able to keep up with my blog and was frequently posting just a picture or a short post because my mind couldn't put together anything more complex. I needed to get new shoes and socks, but I didn't have the energy to put on my existing pairs of shoes and socks to go to the store. My co-workers had gone out for drinks last week and invited me along, but I had turned them down to go home and pour salt water through my nostrils. This was not a life.

I couldn't sit here waiting. I needed to make progress. I had to at least try to escape this cage my body had become. The next day, I sat alone in the parking lot while the woman on the other end of the phone line asked me, "Do you weigh more than three hundred and fifty pounds?" I was relieved that I could finally answer that question with a "no." Otherwise I wouldn't have fit into the MRI machine.

Three days later, I went to an imaging center located next to the hospital and filled out a form stating that I had no shrapnel or metal implants in my body. This was the nicest waiting room yet. The chairs were comfortable—cushy and upholstered in a soft cloth. There were real plants positioned decoratively around the room, not the fake kind with dusty leaves. The fish tank in the corner had fake plants though, as well as a dozen tropical fish. The room was almost absent of scent, as though the air had been highly filtered and conditioned before entering my lungs.

The only thing I didn't like were all the sick, old people. They reminded me that I was going to die someday, and that my body had not-so-secret plans to become wrinkly, slow-moving, and odd-smelling on the way down. A man next to me was breathing through an oxygen tank. He sat near a woman who was so frail that I'd had to hold the heavy wooden door open for her on the way in. I reminded myself that old age was not contagious, or if it was it took decades to take effect. After only five minutes of waiting, I was called back for the test by a blond woman wearing pink scrubs.

I didn't have to change into a gown, but I did have to store my earrings, watch, and any other metal objects in a locker located in a small changing room. Then the tech led me through some wide white corridors that all looked alike, making me feel like a mouse trapped in a maze. I lay down on the table sticking out of the MRI machine, and the technician put a plastic frame over my head that resembled a football player's helmet grill. It was designed to help them align the machine properly with my head.

"Would you like to listen to the radio or watch some TV?" the technician asked me. I responded affirmatively, and she put some headphones over my ears and handed me some clunky goggles to put on my face. It reminded me of a View-Master that I'd played with as a child, but now Pat Sajak and Vanna White were passing in front of my eyes instead of 3-D images of the Empire State Building or safari animals.

The tech reminded me to stay very still, and I almost nodded in response but simply told her "Okay" instead. The MRI machine made loud clacking and buzzing sounds, and I tried hard not to flinch. I couldn't hear the TV that well, but fortunately my eyes could follow along with *Wheel of Fortune* without sound. I wondered if the brain activity occurring while I solved word puzzles would throw off the test results. When my mind wasn't solving the puzzle, it was noticing the patterns in the ruckus. Short, short, short, long, long, long. Short, short, short, long, long, long. I started improvising melodies in my head to go along with the beats. I imagined a stage production of *STOMP!* centered around the MRI machine, where performers smashed their trash can lids together and then lost them to the strong pull of the machine's magnetic field. I was obviously bored out of my mind.

After about fifteen minutes, my table glided out of the machine again. Now the tech needed to inject contrast material into my bloodstream that would highlight my circulatory system in the scan.

"Oh, my veins evidently roll, but I have no idea what that means," I told her before she stuck my arm and failed to tap my vein. She stuck my other arm instead and again failed to hit the vein. Then she tried one more time on the original arm, and yet again, my veins remained vacuum-sealed.

Finally, the tech sought out Sally, a nurse with thirty years of experience, who pierced my vein in one stick. I glanced at the clock on the wall and realized it had taken more time to inject the contrast material than it had taken to do the first part of the scan.

They sent me back into the machine. I started to play *Jeopardy!* but was finished with the test before I discovered what film beat *Citizen Kane* for the Best Picture Oscar in 1942. (Answer: *How Green Was My Valley*.)

"Hi, Jennette. This is Nurse Katie at Dr. Rodgers's office. I'm calling to let you know that your test results came back. You have a . . ." Nurse Katie paused as she tried to properly pronounce the next two words. ". . . venous angioma?" she said with an upward lilt at the end as though it were a question. She then continued as if she were reading a script, which she probably was. "It's in the left hemisphere of your brain. This is a benign malformation of the veins. It typically does not cause headaches and is unlikely to cause any problems, but Doctor Rodgers would like for you to get it checked out just in case."

I promptly called the neurosurgeon who was recommended

in the voice mail, but only after I'd googled the term "venous angioma." Wikipedia agreed with Dr. Rodgers that it was probably nothing to be concerned about. Any fear I did have was drowned out by an excited part of my brain that screamed, *Yes! We finally found something wrong with me!*

Unfortunately, this also meant I had added another task to my long list of things I'd rather not do while in constant pain. This list included pretty much everything. If the headache itself hadn't exhausted me first, all of this testing would have.

At least the neurosurgeon's waiting room was a nice place to relax. It had a fish tank and filtered air, just like the imaging center, but it also had plush, ultramodern chairs. As if I couldn't have guessed it already, brain surgery must pay well.

A bearded gentleman wearing a suit and tie entered the room and sat down after signing in. *Oh my God, he must have a brain tumor,* I thought to myself, feeling sorry for the stranger. I focused intently on my issue of *Good Housekeeping* and tried not to wonder how sick he was, or think about how his wife must put up a brave front for him but secretly cries in the bathroom with the shower running, because they've just bought a house that she won't be able to afford after he dies and, *Wait! Does he think I have a brain tumor, too?* If I didn't have a brain tumor, maybe he didn't either. He might have just hit his head while playing hockey. He might live happily ever after with his wife in the big house after all.

I decided to stop making up a backstory for my fellow patient and focused on my magazine. Even though I doubted I would subscribe to *Good Housekeeping,* it was more interesting than the mommy-centric magazine I'd read while waiting for the MRI or the somewhat shallow girls' magazine I'd skimmed before my CT. Being sick was giving me a good opportunity to catch up on magazines.

"Jennette Foolda?" The nurse called out another common mispronunciation of my name.

"Fulda, like the Fulda Gap in Germany," I told her as if this reference to military trivia would clarify things. She led me to an examination room, where she took my blood pressure, weight, and pulse and left me to wait for the doctor. He came through the door fifteen minutes later.

Dr. Carpenter had a white beard and two patches of hair on either side of his otherwise bald skull. I was reassured by his age, which I gauged as old enough to be very skilled in his field, but not so old as to have gone senile.

"Hello," he said in a soft monotone. He shook my hand somewhat stiltedly, as if he was uncomfortable touching people. He sat down on a swivel stool and opened a manila folder containing my file. "Can you tell me what you're in here for today?" He was all business. No "How's the weather?" or the dreaded "How are you doing?" Usually I hated small talk, but I wanted to feel some sort of connection to this man. I was entrusting him with my brain, which was, if not my most important organ, at least in the top five. Instead, all I felt was the chill as the air-conditioner kicked in.

"I've had a headache for over two months now." I told him about the MRI results, wondering why he didn't know this information already. What were all those goddamn forms for?

"About the headache, what have you tried to treat it? What tests have they done?" he asked as he clicked a ballpoint pen to start taking notes on his file folder.

I stared at my reflection bouncing off his glasses and wondered if deer that were caught in headlights also froze because they couldn't remember their recent medical history. We'd tried Tylenol and Excedrin and all that amateur, over-the-counter bullshit. Then I'd gotten a shot, and then I'd taken the antibiotics. But wait, was that before or after the CT? And what was the name of the migraine pill I'd tried? Hadn't I gotten a few samples of Claritin-D or Allegra-D or something with a D in it, too? I really needed to start writing all this down. This was like playing the alphabet game as a child, where we'd tell each other, "I'm going to the park and I'm taking an apple, a barbecue grill, a corndog, and a donkey" and then taking turns adding one more thing to a list. Only this time it was, "I'm going to the doctor and I'm taking acetaminophen, beta-blockers, a cold compress, and Depakote!"

I told the doctor what I could remember about my recent medical history. He looked up and asked me, "What does the pain feel like?" The monotone of his voice made it sound like he didn't care what my pain felt like, or perhaps he'd seen so much pain that he'd cut himself off from empathizing with every patient for his own protection.

Regardless, it was a good question, yet an extremely difficult one to answer. I hated trying to describe the pain. The more I tried to explain it, the more I realized how ill-suited words were for the task, as though I were trying to paint a portrait of my headache with a zucchini. I couldn't even properly describe where the pain was. Its edges were fuzzy, brushing up against my skull and deep behind my nose. My neck seemed to hurt, too, or was I just imagining that?

It also amazed me that a force so overbearingly destructive and constantly present in my life could be invisible to others. I was stuck in some twisted version of *The Emperor's New Clothes* in which I really did have invisible clothes, only they were woven out of steel wool.

"The pain is on both sides of my head, ranging from here to here," I said as I traced my fingers over my cheekbones, around my nose, and up over my forehead. "I feel pressure there, sort of like an achy muscle, but much worse. You know that scene in *Alien* where the little multi-limbed creature leaps onto a minor character's face right before implanting him with alien spawn? It feels like that."

The doctor did not laugh or even smile at my clearly hilarious analogy, and at that moment I decided I did not like him. Instead, he made some notes and then gave me a drunk driving test, or as he called it, a neurological exam. I had to walk in a straight line on my tippy toes and then on my heels. I had to touch my finger to my nose with one eye closed. I had to follow his pen left and right. Then he whipped out a tuning fork, but before I could ask him where his piano was, he struck the tuning fork on the desk, placed it on my knee and asked if I could feel the vibrations. I could.

At the end of the exam, the doctor told me I was a paradigm of good health and that a venous angioma was nothing to worry about. It meant that my veins in that part of the brain were organized atypically, but that abnormality was normal for me and probably would never have been discovered without the MRI. Then the exam was over, and Dr. Carpenter didn't even walk me out to the front desk.

What was I supposed to do now (besides pay the bill)? Wasn't the doctor supposed to refer me to someone else or tell me to get another test? I needed a project manager for this headache, someone to make my appointments, figure out my insurance, and research doctors and treatments for me. It was certainly a full-time job, and not one a person in constant pain was well qualified for. I had no experience being chronically ill and would not have been hired for this position if it had been advertised in the classifieds.

Not really knowing what to do next, I took my MRI films home and collapsed on the love seat, which creaked loudly. I was surprised it hadn't broken beneath me from all the times I'd collapsed on it this year. I dialed a number on my cell phone.

"Hi, Mom," I greeted my mother as I looked at a photo of her placed on a corner of the coffee table. She had short silver hair and was smiling joyfully at something the photographer must have said. I saw her fairly often outside of a photo frame, too, because she lived in an apartment across town. My younger brother lived even closer, and they were both a good source of love and support, even when I didn't feel like guillotining myself.

"Hi, honey," she replied. "Did you go to the doctor today?"

"Yeah." I gave her the short version of his diagnosis.

"Well, that's good to hear," she said, and then there was a long stretch of silence. "Are you okay?" she asked. Leave it to my mother to notice my despondent mood by the way I was breathing. She always wanted to fix her children's problems, but my headache could not be cured by topping off my car's radiator fluid or hemming my jeans, as she'd done earlier that month.

"Oh . . ." I debated what to say. I could try to put up a strong front for my mother's sake, or I could tell the truth. My upper lip made the decision for me as it started to tremble. I felt my face scrunch up as if to dam the tears, but I didn't have the will to keep up my facade any longer. "I feel awful," I confessed. I started to bawl, and a river of snot dripped onto the receiver. I began to hyperventilate. "I just . . . don't know . . . what . . . to do," I said between breaths. I hadn't cried like this since middle school. I'd never been a drama queen, so it felt odd to be displaying this much emotion so suddenly. The crying made my sinuses feel particularly stuffy, but it was nice to feel a different variety of pain for a change.

"I'm so sorry, honey," my mother said, trying to wrap me in a hug over the telephone line. "Is there anything I can do?"

"No," I told her. There didn't seem to be anything anyone could do, not even the experts.

"I can come over and do your dishes," she offered. Okay, I guess there was one thing she could do. I accepted her offer, and her digitized voice did the best it could to comfort me. "You know, your dad used to have headaches. His brother, your Uncle Jerry, used to get migraines, too, I think."

"Really?" I'd never known this. What other horrible diseases was I going to develop as I aged? I should demand full medical histories from all my relatives immediately.

"You should call him," she told me.

"Yeah . . . I should do that." I didn't want to do that.

More than five years ago my father had told us he was going on a business trip to North Carolina and then never came back. He didn't go to North Carolina either. I'd discovered this in a twenty-two-page letter he'd mailed to my off-campus apartment. Our relationship had been understandably strained after his departure, but we were slowly salvaging what was left of it. I'd accepted that he hadn't been in the best mental health when he'd made the decision to leave, and was trying to forgive him for driving an armored tank through our lives upon his exit.

We had never been close before he left so we were rebuilding our relationship on flimsy ground. I'd seen him a year ago at a funeral, and I had called him on Thanksgiving and Christmas, but that was about it. I emailed him about my headache. Three days later the phone rang, and the caller ID displayed my father's name as a warning. I felt cocoons burst open as butterflies filled my stomach. I picked up the phone and said, "Hi, Dad."

"Hellooooooo!" my father's voice boomed down the phone line in a singsong tone. His manically joyful tenor was probably overcompensation for his own nerves. "I got your email," he said. "So, you have been having headaches?"

"Well, really just one headache." I filled him in on my medical history, now that I'd written it all down to tell whatever doctor I ran into next. He talked about his headaches, which had started in college. He told me about how he'd had to turn off the lights and lie in the dark with his migraines. He recommended I rotate painkillers to prevent rebound headaches caused by withdrawal. He told me how yogurt, ice cream, and chocolate could trigger his episodes. He talked about the autoimmune diseases that occurred in our family, including multiple sclerosis, rheumatoid arthritis, and ITP, a disease that caused a low platelet count in the blood.

We talked for almost an hour. After I finally hung up the phone, my head still ached and I didn't really have any new leads, but at least now my father and I had something to talk about.

3

Trading Truffles for Vicodin

To: Jennette.Fulda@home

From: Karen@DownwardFacingDog

Subject: Yoga Headache Remedy

I'm sure you'll be creeped out by the fact that a stranger is thinking of you while in yoga. But it's a headache remedy that I have doubts you've tried. And mostly it just made me laugh. I genuinely believe that yoga has many beneficial aspects (my joking solution for every problem is to do more yoga), but I'm not one of those crazy yogis.

Have you investigated that the problem may be with your ajna chakra? My teacher mentioned last night that a problem in this area could result in headaches. Apparently doing yoga blindfolded should help, or you should stop looking at bad art, or travel to Thailand.

Karen

I was seriously considering a prescription drug addiction. It sounded like a joke, but it wasn't. My weight-loss memoir was about to come out, and I didn't think it would be good for publicity to continue indulging my chocolate addiction. Ever since the headache had begun three months ago, I'd been sneaking pints of raspberry–chocolate-chip ice cream into my apartment and buying Bavarian custard doughnuts on the sly, assuring myself that it was highly unlikely anyone at the grocery story was a member of the food police.

Chocolate was listed as a possible headache trigger, but I decided the joy it gave me outweighed any possible negative effects it might have. The moment a spoonful of ice cream touched my taste buds, I felt a hit of pleasure that I could no longer find elsewhere in my life. The melting ice cream drowned out the nagging voice of pain that I had to listen to twenty-four hours a day. Eating was literally the only time I felt good. But it had made me gain ten pounds, which was enough to push me up one jeans size.

I was starting to become concerned about my weight but calmed myself by remembering that I'd faced small gains like this before. Once I managed to get rid of the headache, I knew I would have the energy and focus to burn off the extra pounds. I also knew I could not be seen talking about "My Amazing Weight Loss!" when I was secretly stuffing brownies down my throat at night.

I tried alcoholism first. It was easier to buy liquor than narcotics. I drank four shots of vodka straight up, alone, in my apartment after work. This only made my headache worse, as if it were a fire I'd dumped the vodka on. It also led me to broadcast inebriated tweets on Twitter, like "Wheee! Being drunk is fun!" which my co-workers enjoyed taunting me with the next day. At least I hadn't been fired for it. I decided that, sadly, alcoholism wasn't for me.

Prescription drugs seemed to be my next best bet. I had fond memories of the Vicodin I'd gotten after my gallbladder attack several years ago. It had left me in a happy haze, oblivious to the pain in my abdomen. I thought about asking my doctor for some more, but I was afraid of appearing to be a pill-seeker, which, of course, I was.

"I have some pills," my friend Angela told me over the phone. I'd met Angela in college, but unlike most people, we had waited until *after* we graduated to experiment with drugs. "My wisdom tooth became abscessed last week, and I've got almost a whole bottle of Vicodin left."

"Oh my God, would you? Really? I would love you forever!" I told her. "Oh crap, should we be talking about this over the phone? What if the government is listening?"

There was a pause. "I will assume your paranoia is a side effect of the headache," Angela replied.

Two days later she was standing on my front porch, wearing

jeans and an army-green hoodie, rattling a small, cylindrical bottle of pills in my face. "Thanks! I got you something, too," I told her as I picked up a paper bag with her gift inside. She reached in and pulled out a box of chocolate truffles.

"Aw, thanks," she replied as we completed our illicit drug deal with a hug.

I took one pill that night and waited an hour. I didn't feel anything, or rather I still felt like my skull was lined with sandbags. I took another pill. Half an hour later I was kneeling in front of the toilet, afraid I might spew what was left of my lunch into the porcelain bowl. The label had said to take the pills with food, but I'd tossed them into an empty stomach. At least I hadn't tossed them down with vodka. A feeling of light-headed euphoria was floating above the nausea. It was a sensation I remembered from the first time I'd taken Vicodin years ago, but my headache was still grounding my body to the Earth. I felt top-heavy, as though I might fall over at any moment. I got up, put on my pajamas, turned off the lights, and went to bed.

As my ear rested against my pillow, I heard the slow rhythm of my pulse. THUMP . . . THUMP . . . THUMP. I wasn't disturbed by the thumping, but I was petrified by the long gaps between THUMPS. I hit the glow-in-the-dark button on my watch and started counting heartbeats. My pulse was only forty beats per minute. Normally it should be at least sixty beats per minute. What if my heart stopped? Should I go to the ER? There was no way I could afford the ER.

I lay awake in bed for the next hour, hoping that my paranoia was a side effect of the headache. Eventually I fell asleep, and was grateful to wake up in the morning, even if the familiar pain was there to greet me as reliably as the sunrise.

A week later, I was still alive and my heart was beating rather fast as I ran past a man sitting in a lawn chair drinking a Budweiser. About 35,000 other people were jogging along with me, proving that even if thousands of people are doing something, it can still be a bad idea. I had paid the $50 entrance fee for the Indianapolis Mini-Marathon back in September, long before my headache had appeared in February. Now it was May, and my eyes were searching desperately for a water station up ahead, but the only liquid nearby seemed to be the man's beer.

I could have dropped out of my training and given my registered spot to someone else, but I'd told everyone I was going to do it and I wanted to be able to say I'd lost half my weight and then run a half-marathon, even if the idea was half-baked. So I'd pinned the number onto my chest that morning and started running more than thirteen miles. The aching in my shins and my abdomen helped distract me from my headache. The pain in other parts of my body was like a thunderstorm drowning out the irritation of a dripping faucet in my head.

Four hours after I had crossed the finish line and collapsed against a tree, I was greeting guests at my book release party at a local Italian restaurant. I entertained the crowd with a smile and shoved the headache into the darkest corner of my mind. No one mentioned it, and I made sure not to bring it up. I'd stopped blogging about the headache, too, because I was sick of talking about it. I was sick of the way people tilted their heads and scrunched up their faces in sympathy when I told them about the headache. I was sick of hearing "I hope you feel better soon," because it reminded me that I might never get better, either sooner or later, and I was not ready to accept that. I was sick of people telling me what they thought was causing my headache, because they were really just telling me what had been the cause of their own headaches or their friends' headaches. I was sick of being sick.

After the crowd trickled out, I helped my aunts, my cousins, and my mom clean up. I threw some wadded-up paper tablecloths into a trash can my mother was holding. "Do you still have your headache?" she asked.

I looked up at her in surprise. "Yeah. Believe me, if it had gone away I would have thrown another party just for that."

Her eyes looked sad. "Oh, I'm sorry. I couldn't tell. You seemed so energetic. I hoped maybe it had gotten a bit better." I tried not to get mad. I didn't want anyone to know about my headache and I'd pulled it off perfectly, but now I was upset at someone for believing my act. It was easy for people to forget that I was in pain if I wasn't scrunched up in a ball moaning all the time. I didn't want pity, but a bit more understanding wouldn't have made me hurt any worse.

For the next few weeks, I spent my days at work and my evenings working on book promotions. I had only a small window of opportunity when my book was new enough to be considered for magazine stories or blog tours. I powered through the pain, as if I were walking on hot coals, focusing only on getting to the other side. I had worked too hard for too long to let a stupid headache ruin my plans. I wasn't superhuman, though. My work at my full-time job was getting sloppy. I was taking more and more breaks to go sit on the couch in the women's bathroom, trying to avoid heading back to my desk. I wasn't sure how much longer I could do this before I literally collapsed on the floor of the ladies' room, from which I would surely get that bacterial infection I'd been hoping for.

At the beginning of June, I drove to South Bend, traveling the same road I'd been on when the headache had first appeared six years ago, to visit the same friend I had visited then, Cristy. We had been friends since second grade. She'd seen me at my fattest and my thinnest, and now at my healthiest and sickest. I had scheduled a signing at a South Bend bookstore as an excuse to spend time with her. I ended up spending more time with her couch.

"Do you want to go somewhere for lunch?" Cristy asked. I blinked, losing my staring contest with her bookshelf on the opposite wall. My mind felt deep-fried, extra crispy.

"Uh, whatever you want to do," I mumbled. I had sunk into the plush cushions of her microfiber couch the moment I had arrived. Driving for three hours was like knocking over an anthill and daring a hundred little creatures to gnaw on my nerve endings.

Cristy sat down on the couch next to me and pulled her dirty-blond hair into a ponytail. "Well, we could go to the Indian place. There's also a nice Italian restaurant. Or we could just go to Applebee's or T.G.I. Friday's. I think my friend Violet wants to come along, and she's really picky and only eats at T.G.I. Friday's, but don't let that affect your choice."

I paused for a moment, trying to make a decision. I could tell

Cristy was trying to make me happy by giving me several options to choose from, but the variety of choices overloaded my brain. The only words that came out of my mouth were "Sure, whatever." The headache evidently required so much energy to run that I could no longer power the decision-making portion of my mind.

"Do you have another preference?" Cristy asked. "I want to go to a place that has something healthy for you to eat. I don't want to sabotage your diet," she said, unaware that I was doing a very good job of sabotaging my diet without the help of the T.G.I. Friday's dessert menu.

"T.G.I. Friday's sounds fine," I said, summoning up enough strength to remember I'd eaten a tasty salad there a few months ago.

"Okay, but are you sure?" she asked. "I don't want to go there just because of Violet. You're my guest, so pick the place you really want to go." I would have happily eaten grass clippings from the backyard if it had meant I wouldn't have to make this decision.

"What's with your dog?" I asked. Cristy's roommate owned a dachshund-beagle mix named Coco who had been lying in a bed by the TV at the beginning of our conversation. As we'd debated dining options, Coco had gotten up, circled his bed twice, and then trotted to the front door and started whimpering.

"Oh, it's nothing. He's just a bit neurotic and has social anxiety, but we love him anyway," Cristy said. Coco stopped whimpering, walked back around the couch, circled his bed three times, and then lay down. "Nobody's at the door. He just does that all the time," Cristy said. I sat on the couch for twenty more minutes while Cristy called her friends and they debated how many cars we would take to the restaurant and the best route to get there. As predicted, Coco repeated his obsessive-compulsive ritual two more times while Cristy was on the phone.

I couldn't summon the strength to push against gravity and stand up from the couch, so I slid off the cushions and took a kneeling position on the floor instead. I crawled four steps to Coco's bed and scratched behind his ears. He rubbed his head against my hand in response.

"I know, boy," I whispered. "I know."

By the beginning of June, the majority of my book publicity work was done, and I was ready to resume the endless work of investigating my headache. I decided to hire Dr. Fairweather as my neurologist because he specialized in headaches. It said so, right there on the Internet. I did feel like I was hiring him, as if he were a contractor for my head. No one had pointed me where to go next. The neurologist who'd diagnosed my venous angioma had been satisfied to complete his part of the job and had offered no further advice. I'd visited my primary-care physician's office so many times that I couldn't bear to go back there. This case wasn't going to be solved by the doctor with wire-frame glasses. Instead, I determined that a neurologist was the type of doctor I needed to see, so I researched my local options and picked the one I hoped would be best, though it felt as though I were picking numbers out of a lottery bowl. Luckily, my new insurance didn't require that I get a referral first.

Dr. Fairweather's office sent me an admission packet with several pages of forms to fill out, asking all sorts of questions about the history of my headache and where the pain was. They also requested I bring any CT or MRI films with me, so I had to go back to the imaging center and wait twenty minutes in their waiting room next to the fish tank while a tech made copies for me. He finally came out with a huge paper folder the size of a small art portfolio. I tossed it into the backseat of my car and went to my appointment the next day.

Dr. Fairweather's office was downtown in an office park next to a hospital. There was no one else in the waiting room, which was dimly lit because bright lights could trigger migraines. A wall of windows faced onto the parking lot, but the shades were closed, so I couldn't see my car. There wasn't a TV or radio playing in the background, which made the room seem cold and empty. There weren't any of the typical periodicals lying around either, just dozens of copies of the same magazine, which featured stories on different neurological diseases that could destroy your life. Carefully positioned next to the articles were advertisements for prescription drugs to treat those diseases.

I was called back by the nurse, Ginny, who took my pulse, blood pressure, and weight. I sighed at the numbers on the scale, which had been moving in the wrong direction lately. Ginny led me into an examination room. The nurse looked tired, and I asked her if she was okay.

"Oh, I'm fine. I get migraines, and the weather lately sure hasn't helped." I felt bad for Ginny, but I also felt glad that she understood what it was like to have a chronic headache.

"The weather can cause headaches?" I asked.

"Yeah, any sudden change in weather can trigger a migraine. It can be the temperature, or the— Oh, what's it called?" I wasn't sure what phrase Ginny was grasping for, but she found it on her own. "The barometric pressure! That's it. But yeah, people like us who have migraines have brains that don't like change. Our bodies overreact to it. A lot of people have been coming in the last few days for shots," she told me. I envisioned a swarm of tired migraineurs staggering toward the clinic like zombies, chanting, "Need drugs. Aaaargh."

"So, do you get a lot of patients?" I asked.

"Unfortunately, yeah. I believe something like forty-five million Americans have chronic headaches. That's about one in six people."

"Wow," I told her. I'd had no idea that chronic headache problems were that widespread.

Ginny left and I waited. This examination room was unlike the other doctor's offices I'd been in. There was a chair behind a desk facing the chair I sat in. Other than the charts on the walls diagramming veins and nerves in the head, there were no other furnishings. No examination table. No sink or hazardous waste disposal box.

Dr. Fairweather entered the room holding a thick, durable laptop computer. He had kind eyes and greeted me warmly with a smile. He appeared to be fairly handsome, but the room was so dimly lit that we probably all looked more attractive than we were. We reviewed my history and he tapped notes into his computer. My medical records, sent over from my primary-care physician, filled in many of the details of my treatments. I pulled out of my purse a list of questions, written on a notepad, that I didn't want to forget to ask.

"What are the treatment approaches for headaches like this?"

"There are two ways we attack headaches," he said. "First, when you have a headache we try to abort it. Your headache has been stuck in a cycle, so we'll try to break that cycle. Once we've broken the cycle, we'll try preventatives, which are the other way of treating headaches, by stopping them from happening at all." In just one minute he'd told me more about headache treatments than all my other medical professionals combined. This was promising.

"What can cause a headache like this?" I asked. "Is it vascular? Is my nervous system on the fritz?" Dr. Fairweather pointed to the diagrams on the walls as he explained different theories about the mechanics of headaches. Originally, a tension headache like mine was thought to be caused by tension in the muscles around the head. These days it was believed tension headaches were more complex than that, and perhaps not caused by muscle tension at all. Some people believed migraines were caused by the dilation of blood vessels in the head. Others believed neurotransmitters in the brain had something to do with how pain signals were transferred because medications that acted on these chemicals could bring relief.

By the end of our conversation, I decided that if I were to draw a map depicting our knowledge of different fields of medicine, the section about headaches would say, "Here be dragons." An x-ray could look at my bones and a CBC panel could analyze the contents of my blood, but there wasn't a good way to look at what my nerve cells were doing. I couldn't think of any celebrities who were campaigning for headache research funding, so I doubted my disease was getting the financial backing it would need for scientists to find answers to my questions anytime soon.

"I'm going to prescribe a five-day IV drug treatment for you," Dr. Fairweather said. My eyebrows rose in surprise. That sounded rather serious. The last time I'd had an IV, I'd also had an organ removed.

"What does that involve?" I asked.

"You can have it administered at home, by an infusion pharmacy. They'll send the supplies to your house, and a nurse will come over to start the IV and show you how to administer the treatment."

This sounded hard-core. This was exactly what I needed. No more pills and diet changes. We were going to inject the medication directly into my bloodstream (assuming that the nurse could find my tiny, rolling veins). I was slightly surprised that all I had to do to get this treatment was to complain about a headache that no one could technically prove existed. None of my tests indicated that there was anything wrong with me (besides the abnormal, yet benign cluster of veins in my brain). For all they knew, I could have been making the whole thing up.

It was nice that Dr. Fairweather trusted me. I felt better simply talking to him. He explained things in a way I could understand, and his gentle facial expressions made me feel he was empathetic to my plight. He didn't blame me for my pain and didn't tell me I was imagining it. Better yet, we had a plan of action. I had started to wonder if this headache was ever going to go away, but now I had hope that it just might.

"Thank you," I told him, and then I checked out at the front desk. The nurse there told me that the infusion pharmacy would call me either today or tomorrow to schedule the treatment.

I left the doctor's office and drove toward a coffeehouse on the other side of town. My old friend from high school, Leah, was in town for a conference, and we'd arranged to meet there that evening to catch up. Leah stood inside the café, wearing a stylish green skirt and a patterned blouse that flattered her olive skin. I was wearing jeans and a T-shirt and felt like a schlub standing next to her. Keeping up my appearance hadn't been my first priority lately, but I hadn't felt self-conscious about it until now. A flutist and a man with a bongo were playing music loudly inside, so we went outside with our iced coffees and sat at the stone tables on the patio.

"How are things with you and Casey?" I asked, playing with the green plastic straw in my drink. She'd been dating Casey for more than a year and was head over heels for him. I could tell by the way she glowed whenever she talked about him.

"I want to marry him," she replied softly, as if she were telling me her most precious secret.

"Wow, it's that serious?" I asked her.

"I feel like it's time. I finally feel like I'm at a time in my life when I'm ready to be married." Leah was about to start her third year of medical school. Casey worked at the same hospital as she did. She took a sip from her soy latte. "What about you?"

I started to laugh, my typical defense reflex. "Ha! No, I have no desire to be married right now, or to have kids. I feel like I just learned how to take care of myself, you know? And even that's not going so well right now."

"I didn't mean marriage," she said. "I was just wondering, any romantic prospects?"

This was a topic of conversation I avoided like lima beans. I was twenty-seven years old and I'd never had a serious boyfriend. I knew this was weird, but I still hadn't made an effort to do anything about it. I'd always been fat and shy, so boys didn't flock to me and I avoided them. I didn't have many male friends either, all of which was probably linked to my father and how distant he'd been during my childhood. Now, I evidently had a problem forming intimate relationships, but if asked, I would genuinely tell people I was happy as I was. However, even if a fish didn't need a bicycle, that didn't mean it couldn't have fun cycling sometime.

"I . . . uh, have been thinking about maybe doing online dating or something," I told her and then quickly shoved the green straw to my face for a long sip.

"It's time, Jennette," she said. She was right. I knew she was right. I wanted to pretend she was wrong, but she was right.

Later we hopped into my car so I could give her a lift back to her hotel.

"Jennette, you have MRI films in your backseat," she said.

"Yes. Yes, I do."

That night I turned on my computer and went to Match.com. I started to fill out the free profile but stopped when I got to a screen with dozens of fields for all my hobbies, favorite TV shows, and pets. I felt more overwhelmed than when I was filling out complicated medical admission forms. I would get back to this later. Of course I would. Then I would also figure out how to tell any possible suitors about the loose skin left from my weight loss, not to mention my chronic headache. Then I'd finish the job by telling them about all my poor character traits and chatting at length about my cats.

I turned off the computer, knowing I would never finish the profile. I would probably have to date several people before I found somebody I liked. When was I supposed to find the time to do that? My evenings consisted of dates with my pillows. A boyfriend would also expect me to venture outside of my apartment and go to dinner with him, or at least see a movie. I preferred lying on my bed in a dark room to watching a movie in one. I didn't have the energy for a boyfriend. And who would want to date me? I had MRI films in my backseat. I was damaged goods, and it was uncertain if I'd ever be repaired.

4

Intravenous Drugs with Nurse Joan

To: Jennette.Fulda@home

From: Michael@SpiritOrbs

Subject: Tension Headaches

I enjoyed your website and its humor. Of particular interest were your two blogs on this email's subject.

You aren't likely to believe the cause of your headaches, so consider this email and my website as seeds (an idea) for your mind. At an appropriate time in the future, the cause will make itself known to you. So, here I go. Tension headaches, like many so-called neurological maladies that science can't explain, are not actually physiological. They are of supernatural origin. To put it in a nut shell, that thick-headed, tension feeling you've been having is caused by a spirit. Please, don't hang up just yet, as it gets even more interesting. Those with tension and other types of chronic headaches, where science hasn't identified a cause, are the saints spoken of in the scriptures. Think for a moment about the artwork you may have seen depicting the saints, and their halos. Those halos are generally thought to be artistic decorations indicating holiness. In actuality, those halos are spirits, and are about the heads of saints for reasons of logic and science. The feeling of such a spiritual presence is exactly what you and many describe as the symptoms of a tension headache. Not believable? As indicated above, this email is merely a seed. Has your neurologist helped you?

Please come to my website and see what else I've written, as well as some of the photographic evidence presented there. Enjoy, and as a saint, I hope you keep up all of your good deeds!

"Hi, I'm Nurse Joan from the infusion pharmacy. Are you Jennette?"

"Yes, that's me," I said as I opened the door for the gray-haired woman dressed in a light green blouse and khakis. Her clothing surprised me. I thought she would be wearing a uniform, but I suppose a cute, white nurse's outfit with a dainty hat would have made her look like a singing telegram. Nurse Joan shuffled past me into my one-bedroom apartment. She held only her purse and a small, blue canvas bag the size of a makeup kit.

"Did the warehouse drop off the IV pole and your medication?" she asked.

"Yes," I said as I closed the door. I walked across my living room toward the shiny, silver IV pole and the huge white garbage bag of medication and supplies that the delivery man had dropped off earlier in the day. I'd had to leave work early to accept the delivery and to be home during Joan's on-call hours. "There's a lot of . . . stuff . . . here," I said as I looked quizzically into the bag. "Stuff" was the only word I had to describe most of the unfamiliar medical supplies inside, all wrapped in sterilized plastic. I turned to see Nurse Joan's clear blue eyes surveying my apartment with the determination of someone about to set up a MASH unit.

"The kitchen looks like a good spot to start your IV. There's lots of light." She set her bag down on my kitchen counter. There were three wooden, high-backed barstools lined up beneath the counter, which formed a waist-high wall between the kitchen and the living room.

"Works for me," I said. If I started to gush blood, it would be easier to clean it off the tile than the carpet. I hopped up on a barstool facing her as she rummaged through the large plastic bag. Joan pulled out three items: a catheter, extension tubing, and a kit to start the IV.

My large white garbage bag of supplies contained multiple duplicates of all three items, along with syringe caps, mini-spike dispenser pins, and other items I would know the names of only after I had read the labels. All of it was individually wrapped. All of it was sterile.

It was clear that modern medicine single-handedly kept the plastics industry in business.

"I need to wash up first," she said. "Do you have soap?"

I grabbed a bottle of watermelon-scented liquid soap from the bathroom. I wished I had something less cute, perhaps with the word "antibacterial" on it, which would seem more medicinal than a bottle with a juicy watermelon on the label. Nurse Joan washed up in the kitchen sink.

"Have you ever done a home IV treatment before?" she asked me as the bubbles frothed over her thumbs.

"No," I replied, somewhat disturbed when she dried her hands on my crusty kitchen towel.

"First off, I'll start your IV, which means I'll be inserting a tube into your veins that is about six inches long, all in all."

"You're going to insert six inches of tubing into my veins?" I asked, slightly panicked.

"No, no, no," she responded quickly. "The part in your vein is only about an inch or two long and it's really narrow. It's connected to the wider piece that is six inches long."

I released a breath I didn't know I was holding. "Okay, that sounds better." Actually, it sounded freaky, but it sounded a little less freaky than what I'd first imagined, which made it seem better in comparison.

"That contraption will remain in your arm during all five days of this treatment. You'll hook up your medication to a long piece of tubing that will screw onto the cap at the end of the tube in your arm. You'll understand this better when I show it to you. You're doing a five-day round of drugs, so I'll show you how to do it today, and the next four days you'll be doing it yourself."

"Okay," I said. Nurse Joan had presumably gone to an accredited school for several years to learn how to do this, but now I was going to take a crash course in my kitchen. Joan ripped open the IV starter kit. Then she reached for my arm, but paused as her forefinger rubbed up and down a shiny, faded mark near the inside of my elbow. "What's this?" she asked. I was suddenly embarrassed and then, just as suddenly, concerned that she would think it was a scar from a suicide attempt.

"Oh, that's just a stretch mark. I used to weigh almost four hundred pounds." I tossed the sentence off like this was no big deal. I'd talked about it so much by now that it didn't seem like a big deal anymore.

"Wow, really?" she said in awe as she still held my arm. The intimate contact made me feel awkward. "How did you lose it?" I mentally inserted subtitles under her face that translated the real question she was asking: "Did you have weight loss surgery?"

"Just diet and exercise. It took a little over two years." I really didn't want to talk to Nurse Joan about this. I wanted to be a healthy, happy twenty-something who had left work early to share drinks with my friends at a rock concert. Instead, I was a sick, sad twenty-something who had left work early to share weight-loss tips with a thin nurse next to my kitchen sink.

It didn't really matter who I was talking to because I was completely talked out about weight loss. I'd blogged about my weight for three years, then spent another year writing a memoir about it, and I'd just spent two months answering the same questions over and over again to promote the book. The only thing reasonably positive about my recent weight gain was that it meant I might not have to talk about "My Amazing Weight Loss!" ever again. Regardless, I knew I didn't want to be that large again. The only thing worse than weighing almost four hundred pounds was losing two hundred pounds and then gaining it back. That would be worse than never losing it at all. If that happened, my greatest success would become my greatest failure.

"That's amazing, hon," Nurse Joan complimented me. "Good for you."

I tried to act as if I cared what Nurse Joan thought of my weight loss. "Thanks," I murmured simply. I eyed two large posters of my book cover that were turned against the wall near the bookcase. I'd used those at my book release party and book signings and wasn't sure what to do with them now. It seemed egotistical to hang them on the wall, so I'd left them lying around the floor instead. Then my pupils flicked to the stack of complimentary copies of my book in the other corner. *Please, please, don't let her notice them,* I thought. I would rather discuss the regularity of my bowel movements than talk about the glycemic index one more time. I wanted this to be over as quickly as possible and for my home to be my own again.

"So, where are you from?" I asked, trying to steer the conversation toward another topic.

"Brownsburg," she replied, as she took the tourniquet and wrapped it around my right arm. Joan tapped my arm near my elbow as though she were sending Morse code. "Turn your arm a little, hon," she requested as I started to roll it to the left. "No, the other way," she muttered and took matters into her own hands, literally, by gently twisting my arm the other way.

"Do you get faint?" she asked immediately. "I don't want you falling off the stool and cracking your skull open."

Neither did I. It would only make the headache worse. "No, I just get a bit queasy sometimes. I don't like to look at blood."

"Let me know if you start to feel faint," she said, as I stared intently in the opposite direction at a lamp. I felt the warm pressure of her fingers on my arm, then the sting of the needle. I waited. Nothing came up my throat. Nothing came out of my arm either.

"Your veins sure are tiny," she said.

"Sorry," I apologized, promising myself that if I ever got married, it would be to a man with large veins so we could spare our children this misery. We waited a few more moments.

"Well, it's in, but no blood is coming out. We'll have to try again," she said. "Sorry, I pride myself in getting it in one stick."

"It's okay," I lied. Even though I was tired and frustrated by how slowly this was going, I tried to exude a pleasant and positive facade. I knew from my experiences with supermarket cashiers and bank tellers that I got better service from people if I was nice to them. Yet I worried that my overcompensation might make me sound way more chipper than someone in pain should. I didn't want to become a whiner, but neither did I want to undermine the signs that hinted at the true impact my disease had on me. I made a mental note to act more downbeat.

Joan pulled out another IV start kit. "Are you feeling okay?"

"Yeah, I'm fine," I said between deep breaths.

"Let's try this on the couch," she said. "The counter is too high. I need you to be lower. And I don't want you cracking your skull open on the floor." I bet injuring a patient didn't look good on a nurse's employment record.

We got up and I sat on the couch, pulling out a pillow on which to place my arm. So much for blood on the tiles. Hopefully this treatment wasn't going to cost me my renter's deposit in bloodstained carpeting. Nurse Joan placed a paper drape on top of the pillow and underneath my arm. She turned one of the adjustable lamp heads toward us to provide more lighting, giving my arm center stage in the spotlight. She stuck me again and this time the IV took. She taped it down to my arm with a large, clear sticker. I now had a six-inch length of clear tubing sticking out of my arm near my elbow.

"Okay, do you have a table?"

"Uh, yeah. I have a TV tray behind the couch."

Joan grabbed the table and set it up in front of me. She laid out several syringes, caps, and other medical paraphernalia. The small TV tray wasn't big enough to hold everything, so she kept some of the materials in the bag. Java Bean, my black cat, pounced into the room.

"Hold up a sec. Let me put my cat in the other room."

"You don't have to do that," Nurse Joan said. Really? I'd only had medical procedures done in sterile white hospitals. Now cats were skittering about while we plunged metal into my flesh on the couch like we were slicing raw chicken. I had read that some rural Russian hospitals kept felines around to kill the rats, but I didn't think that was the preferred model for medical cleanliness.

"My cat likes to jump at dangling objects. I don't want him ripping my IV out." I got up from the couch, picked up Java Bean, and locked him in the bathroom before sitting down again. My other cat was asleep in the corner and showed no interest in me or the woman sticking me with a sharp object.

Nurse Joan rolled my office chair in front of the couch. I wasn't sure what piece of furniture she was going to hijack next. She pulled out a rectangular plastic bag filled with clear liquid that had a circular metal cap on the bottom. The bag contained Keppra, an anticonvulsant that sometimes alleviates headaches. She hung it on the IV pole and inserted a thirty-inch piece of tubing into the bottom.

Joan then reached into my supply bag to pull out two small bottles of clear liquids. "The procedure is to flush with saline, do the treatment, flush with saline, and then flush with Heparin, okay?" No, it was not okay, but I sensed that was not an option. Heparin was a blood thinner that prevented clotting. I only knew that because the drug had killed several babies in the neonatal intensive care unit at a hospital downtown last year when they had accidentally given the kids adult-size doses of the medicine. I knew that the chemical was harmless when handled correctly, but it scared me to be using medication that could kill someone if misused.

"Don't touch the top of the bottle," Nurse Joan said emphatically, as if she were instructing a small child not to touch the hot stove. "If you touch it, it might get infected. If bacteria gets into your blood system, you could become seriously ill or die." Dear God, why were they trusting me to do this on my own? Joan reached into the bag to grab an alcohol swab. There were enough of them in my bag to disinfect the women's bathroom at work. "If you do touch it, use one of these alcohol swabs to clean it."

Nurse Joan tapped Morse code on the side of the syringe this time, either to send secret messages about the dangers of bacteria or to remove air bubbles. I remembered a young adult novel I'd read as a child where the villain had tried to kill a boy by injecting a syringe full of air into his veins to stop his heart. I asked Nurse Joan if bubbles in my medication could do that. "No. It's okay if there are a few small bubbles in there. You can never get all the bubbles out. One girl called me after a treatment worried about the bubbles, but a few small bubbles won't kill you."

Nurse Joan then attached the Keppra to my IV and released the roller clamp on the thirty-inch piece of tubing to start the treatment. I gazed in fascination at the odd array of tubing and medication connected to my body.

"I noticed you didn't write anything down," she said. I felt like a student being called out by the teacher for not taking notes in class. "Can you remember all this?"

"Yeah, I think I got it," I said. There was no way I would remember all of this.

"You should write this down," she said. Joan pulled out a folder, grabbed a pen, and sat at my kitchen counter. "I'll write out the instructions on the back of this piece of paper."

I stared at the IV bag. The only way I could tell that the Keppra was draining into my veins was by watching the drip in the small air chamber at the top of the tubing.

"I prefer not to insert an IV where your arm bends because it doesn't last as long. All the movement can cause it to come out. You might have to call me to insert it again. If I'm not on call, another nurse will do it."

"Okay."

"Do you think you'll be able to start the other four bags of Keppra yourself?" she asked.

"Yeah, I can handle it."

"I'll start the bags for you."

Joan prepared the bags of medication by attaching a thirty-inch piece of tubing to each one. "You have to keep these in the fridge, as well as the Heparin and the saline once you've opened them." She opened up the fridge door. "I'll put them on top of the eggs."

"I'll try not to make a blood thinner omelet," I joked, hoping she'd laugh. I wanted to lighten the mood of the conversation and steer us away from topics such as fatal bacterial infections. There was silence. Nurse Joan didn't even let out a snort. She sat down at the kitchen counter instead.

"Let me know if you feel dizzy or nauseated or anything like that. I'll stay for the rest of this treatment to make sure you don't have a bad reaction. I have paperwork to fill out anyway."

"What happens if I have a bad reaction?" I asked.

"There's an anaphylaxis kit in the bag," she replied. My younger brother had one of those that we were supposed to use if he ever accidentally ate shellfish. I wasn't sure how to use it, and I doubted the drug overdose scene in *Pulp Fiction* served as a reliable tutorial. I figured Nurse Joan would show me how to use it if necessary, probably right after criticizing my own technique.

I sat on the couch, acutely aware of how odd my life had become. The headache had invaded every aspect of my life, including the sanctity of my home. It was amazing how one simple thing, a headache, could cause a chain reaction in my life that eventually led to me sitting on my couch, watching anticonvulsant medication drip into my veins, while a strange woman did paperwork at my kitchen counter. It was as if someone had set off a long chain of dominoes, one failed treatment toppling over to bump into the next failed treatment. Was this the last domino in my chain? Or were we just getting started? After thirty minutes, I suspected the latter because my headache didn't seem any better or worse.

"You shouldn't get the IV in your arm wet, so if you take a shower, tape some Saran Wrap around it or take a bath and keep that arm outside of the water. If the treatment gives you any strange side effects, call me."

"What kind of side effects could there be?" I asked, regretting the question before it had left my mouth. I could only stay awake at night worrying about side effects I knew about, so ignorance might be bliss. Yet I couldn't quell my curiosity. I decided it was in the best interest of my health to stay informed. Nurse Joan read a list of possible side effects from the drug information sheet. They included dizziness, drowsiness, and headache. How could headache be a possible side effect for a treatment for headache? Would the drug cure my headache only to replace it with a new one?

"What's the weirdest side effect you've encountered?" I asked, because I am a paranoid masochist.

"I had one girl who got horrible migraines. She was on a different drug than you're on. She walked into the hallway of her apartment and suddenly couldn't remember where she was or how to get home. That's called *jamais vu.* Everything familiar to you seems unfamiliar. She eventually figured out how to use the phone, and I told her to stop treatment immediately." She continued filling out the paperwork. "But that's rather rare."

Jamais vu sounded simultaneously frightening and fascinating. I'd never done drugs (other than the illicit pill popping). I'd never even smoked a cigarette. I was slightly intrigued by the bizarre mental state people experienced on psychotropic drugs, but I cared too much about my brain cells to try it myself. It would be interesting to experience the high without the guilt, claiming that my doctor made me do it.

After forty-five minutes the IV bag was empty. The last stream of liquid flowed to the bottom of the tubing and stopped about six inches from the end. "Hmmm, that dripped a little faster than what we were going for," Joan said. I was simply grateful this ordeal would be over fifteen minutes sooner.

"Oh, well. I feel okay. My headache is still here, but I remember how to use a phone and I know where I am."

"That's good."

Nurse Joan supervised me as I unscrewed the IV bag from my elbow, flushed it with saline, and then flushed it again with Heparin. When I was done, I looked at the six-inch tube dangling out of my arm and asked, "Uh, what do I do about this?"

"Do you have an old sock?" I had dozens of medical materials in my supply bag, all individually wrapped in sterile packaging, and now I needed to find an old sock.

"Yeah, I have some under the sink." I grabbed a sock from my bag of cast-offs and old gigantic underwear that I used as rags. Nurse Joan cut off the end so only the elastic cuff remained. She put it on my arm, placed the plastic tubing over the bottom half of the cuff, and then rolled the top over, holding the tubing snug in a pocket.

"That's very high-tech," I said.

Nurse Joan organized my supply bag before she left, grouping all the supplies I would need for the treatment in one bag and stuffing other materials, like the extra IV kits and the anaphylaxis kit, in another. Then she gathered up her things. "If you need anything, just call my cell phone. If you can't get me, you can call the number in your folder." I could tell she cared about doing her job well. I appreciated that, even if her hovering annoyed me and I suspected she thought me incompetent.

"Thanks," I said.

I shut the door and collapsed on the love seat in my usual style. There was blood backing up in the tubing on my arm, but Joan had explained that it was normal. Hypothetically, I could now inject anything directly into my veins. When I'd been morbidly obese, I'd joked about mainlining sugar, but if I had a bottle of corn syrup, I could actually do it. And then die. If not from the sugar then from a horrible infection caused by not efficiently wiping every surface with rubbing alcohol.

Sometimes the cure was worse than the disease, and I had to wonder if this treatment was worth the risk. I felt like I was a breath away from kissing danger. When I was a child riding in the backseat of the car, I had once realized I could open the door at any moment and fall to my death. The only thing stopping me was myself. The more I had thought about it, the more I had felt compelled to open the door, not because I wanted to but because I felt I had to.

I tried not to think about the tube sticking out of my arm. If I thought about the plastic inside my veins, I began to imagine I could feel it there. I pushed away the fear, stuffing it behind the couch with the TV tray. The risk *was* worth it. A cure was worth spending $2,000 on an MRI. It was worth turning my arm into a pincushion. If this treatment didn't work, I was prepared to learn what else wellness was worth.

I pressed the button to turn on the TV, trying not to feel the muscle in my forearm tensing to complete the action, trying not to think of the IV that would be there for four more days. Pat Sajak and Vanna White were on TV, as if they wanted to bear witness to all my medical treatments. I closed my eyes and sank into the ever-present haze of my pain.

• • •

The next day, my co-worker Dave walked over to my desk while I was typing. His hair was oily and slightly mussed, as usual. I looked up to see what he wanted.

"Oh my God, is that blood?" he asked.

I quickly glanced at my inner elbow, afraid that my IV had slipped out. Thankfully, it was still in place, but some blood had backed up into the plastic tube, which was clearly visible because I was wearing a short-sleeved shirt.

"Yeah, that's normal," I said in the same tone I would have used to tell him where the printer was. Dave suddenly looked pale and walked away without posing the question he'd come over to ask.

I liked wearing the IV on my arm. Now everyone could see my sickness. I no longer had an invisible illness, but one I displayed proudly, written in blood. No one at my book release party had known I was in pain, but now I wore a red badge of honor, memorializing my five months of duty. When I'd been morbidly obese, I had been embarrassed that everyone could see my problem. I'd wanted a disguise so no one would know how fat I'd become. Now I wanted everyone to know what I was enduring. There was less shame in this because it seemed to be without blame, whereas most people assigned fault to me for my obesity problem. I didn't want pity for my headache, just understanding, and maybe a hug.

I was particularly happy that it was Dave who had noticed the blood leaking out of my body. Dave liked to complain about things that I wished were the worst of my problems. It was still before lunchtime, but he'd already complained about his daily commute, whined about the price he'd have to pay to upgrade his iPhone, and bemoaned the fact that his maid service hadn't cleaned his bathroom mirror. It was only fear of litigation that kept me from leaping over my desk and beating Dave to death with his shiny MacBook Pro while screaming, "You think you've got problems? I'll give you some bleeping problems!"

My gaze shifted to Elliot, who was working at the desk next to mine. Elliot's brother had been badly injured in a car wreck a few months ago, and his mother had been in and out of the hospital with heart problems. He didn't complain about it, though, and you would never have known about his family's difficulties from looking at him. Elliot sat opposite Sarah, who had been coming into work later and later and had mumbled something to me about insomnia, but I wondered if there was something else going on. As for me, even if I'd never gotten my headache, I'd still have had the invisible experience of losing two hundred pounds, which no one would have known about unless they fixated on the extra flesh that dangled from my upper arms. I could only guess about what was going on in the personal lives of my co-workers that I couldn't see in the expressions on their faces.

I was glad my disease was visible now, at least for this week. I had been concerned that my co-workers might think I was faking my illness and label me a slacker and a pathological liar. They'd only known me for a month before my headache began, so to them I'd always been the girl with a headache, an identity I had trouble embracing. The word "sick" could easily be confused with "lazy" or "weak," adjectives I did not want to see on my performance review next year. My boss got migraines a few times a year, so he had been understanding about granting me sick days, but I hated having to request even a half day off. If I'd had the headache before I'd been hired, I wasn't sure if I would have disclosed the disease. I had kept my boss in the loop about my doctor's appointments because I hadn't known it was going to become a chronic problem. I was probably being overly critical of myself, but I didn't feel as though I were pulling my weight around the office. Did my co-workers secretly think the same thing?

Last month we'd launched a redesign of our company's web site. Everyone was expected to stay late to oversee the transition, but by nine in the evening I had been bent over in my chair, holding my head in my hands, trying not to cry from the pain. I had been a completely useless bag of flesh, not the hardworking web designer I wanted to be.

"Do you need to go home?" my boss's boss had asked. He had been walking by, but stopped at my desk after seeing the expression of agony on my face. I had hesitated for a moment, not wanting to get a reputation as a slacker, but knowing I wouldn't be able to do any more work that evening.

"Yes, thank you," I had told him as I gathered up my things and left for the parking garage. I made it to the second red light on the way home before the tears I'd been choking back finally swelled out of my eyes. My breathing became jagged as I bawled uncontrollably. What if I got fired? How would I pay my medical bills without insurance? COBRA was too expensive for me to afford without a salary.

I had walked into the office the next day and asked Dave how late they had stayed that night. "Oh, we were probably here until one in the morning," he said. "How's your headache?" he asked.

"Eh, about the same," I told him.

"I know what would help. We should move the foosball table right next to your desk," he joked with a smile. "All that noise will surely help you out." I laughed along with him but wondered how much resentment simmered underneath the sarcasm. Now with the IV sticking out of my arm, I could literally wave off any quips before they could leave my co-workers' mouths.

That evening, I chatted with my mom, who let me know that everyone in her prayer group had said a prayer for me the night before. I told her to thank them for me, and then I sat down with my Keppra cocktail kit to start the second treatment. After setting out some syringes on the TV tray, I paused, like someone stumped halfway through a crossword puzzle. I sighed. Remembering all the times my mother had told me to wear a jacket, and all the times I'd realized she was right as I stood shivering at the bus stop, I reluctantly pulled Nurse Joan's handwritten instructions out of the bag. They were in cursive. I didn't know anyone wrote in cursive anymore.

As per her instructions, I carefully filled the syringes with saline and Heparin, but one of them rolled off the TV tray onto the carpet. I thought of how infrequently I vacuumed and how bad the litter box smelled when my cats stepped out of it, scattering tiny fecal particles onto the carpeting. I could practically see the life-threatening bacteria jumping onto the end of the plastic vial. I got an alcohol swab and wiped the nozzle tip as if my life depended on it, because it probably did.

I connected the syringe of saline to my IV and started to push the cool liquid into my veins. Blood pooled on my skin at the insertion point of the IV. As Nurse Joan had predicted, the IV had been jostled sometime during the day, perhaps when I was typing on the computer or when I grabbed a box of cereal off the top shelf.

I pulled at the edge of the clear sticker holding my IV in place, removing it from my skin excruciatingly slowly and painfully so I wouldn't disturb the tubing more than I already had. It felt like I was waxing my inner elbow. After I threw out the sticker, I was able to slide the narrow, plastic tubing up and out of my vein in a surprisingly smooth and painless motion. I held the IV up in front of my eyes, gawking at the inch of narrow tubing that had been inside me.

"Hi," I said into the phone. "I need someone to come reinsert an IV."

"Okay," said the infusion pharmacy employee on the other end of the line. "Are you in a lot of pain?"

I'd been expecting him to ask for my address, not inquire about my pain levels. The question he posed made me feel sorry for all the people who called in and answered yes. "No, I have a constant low-grade headache. I can wait. I just need to do a treatment tonight."

"All right. I can get a nurse over to your house in about an hour."

Eighty minutes later, Nurse Karen walked through my door. She looked about the same age as Nurse Joan but had distinct laugh lines on her face, which made me hope she had a better sense of humor than her colleague. She found a vein on the top of my left hand, above my wrist, and inserted the IV there. The pain of the needle lingered much longer this time in my thin, sensitive skin. "Now sign this, so I get paid," she said with a conspiratorial grin.

I thanked her as she walked out the door. She'd driven half an hour from the east side of town to assist me, and I felt bad about having bothered her. I hated inconveniencing people for my sake, so much so that I even bagged my own groceries at the store. I would have inserted the IV myself if I had known how.

I pushed saline into my IV and this time it hurt. I could feel every molecule of the liquid bulging out against my small vein, but at least there was no blood leaking out of my skin.

After five days of the IV treatment, I had not developed an infection, nor had I needed to summon Joan or Karen to reinsert the IV. I felt as though I had gained enough medical skills to convincingly play a nurse on television. I was also in possession of an anaphylaxis kit, enough latex gloves to dye fifty T-shirts, and tons of medical tape, all paid for by my health insurance.

I also still had a headache.

The intravenous drugs didn't do shit, but the pint of ice cream in the fridge made me feel better. I wished I could have gotten my health insurance company to pay for mint-chocolate-chip ice cream, which worked far better than a Keppra cocktail.

5

Blood, Tears, No Sweat

To: Jennette.Fulda@home

From: Ali@MojoRepo

Subject: No more recipes, no more weight loss blog—what happened?

Hi PastaQueen,

I have been following your blog since 2006 and never ever posted or send a message. (It's got to be some kind of a record for never responding) but i bought your book. :-)

So, i know with your headache and all, that is your priority.

But i feel you lost your MOJO. you know, you dont post any recipes, no more encouraging blogs about weight loss? What happened to the happy upbeat PQ? did someone exchange her with a bad new version? (I was trying to put the analogy of Microsoft's versions but i am just not a great writer)

So i am emailing just to say cheer up, a lot of worse things can happen and to say, you go girl..

~cheers

Ali

To: Jennette.Fulda@home
From: Emily@Apology
Subject: Perspective

hey there—

was thinking of you last week. read your post about chronic pain and have to admit i was all. . . . hmmpf a headache how can that be chronic pain? walk a mile in my shoes with my crapped out knee and then talk about not wanting to workout and have it drag on your life . . .

and then i got ill with an upper urinary tract infection. high temperature, back pain, vomiting and the worst.headache. ever. and now i get it, if your headache is even half, no a tenth of what i had last week then man i'm impressed and sorry you are going through this. the headache was the last thing to go after a week and half of being really ill and when i woke up yesterday and it was gone i felt like i had my life back.

i wish you had yours back. i'm sorry i silently snarked at your post. just wanted to get that off my chest.

Independence Day came and went, but I wasn't feeling very independent. I continued to be led around by the headache, which took me back to Dr. Fairweather's office. After the Keppra treatment, I sat in the dark examination room opposite the doctor, watching as he typed on his laptop to prescribe another IV treatment, this time a three-day course of Depakote.

Both Depakote and Keppra were drugs that the federal Food and Drug Administration (FDA) had approved for epilepsy, but they had off-label usage for headaches. That meant doctors had noticed the drug helped treat headaches, but that was not the originally intended use for the drug. Nor had sufficient studies been done to prove the effectiveness of the drug for treating that particular symptom. Thus, if you read the label for the medication, it would not mention headaches anywhere unless they were a side effect of the drug. The medications had been tested on humans and were deemed safe to use, but because the treatment was off-label, the drug companies that manufactured the drugs could not advertise them as headache treatments.

The majority of medications that were prescribed for headaches were prescribed off-label. Only a few drugs had been specifically approved as headache treatments. I wasn't sure if that was because of lack of funding, lack of interest, or lack of a big-name celebrity spokesperson for headaches.

None of this really mattered because the Depakote didn't do anything either. The paranoid part of my brain speculated that the infusion pharmacy was secretly replacing the drugs with saline and embezzling the profits, but I knew this was unlikely. The drugs just hadn't worked. Any hope Dr. Fairweather had given me was now gone, just like the medicine in the plastic bags.

"Let's try Topamax," he told me at my next appointment. Topamax was a headache preventative that was also used to treat epilepsy, bipolar disorder, and depression.

"Sure, fine, whatever," I mumbled, still somewhat depressed by the number I'd seen on the scale when the nurse had weighed me before the appointment. Considering the amount of ice cream I'd been eating in the evenings, it shouldn't have been so surprising. "What are the possible side effects?" I asked him.

"Yadda, yadda, yadda—" (stuff I don't remember) "—and possible weight loss."

My face lifted and I replied, "Okay," way faster than I should have.

Dr. Fairweather gave me a sample bottle of the medication and wrote out instructions on how to gradually increase the dosage of the Topamax over the next month. I came home with my mood slightly lifted, as it often was before a new treatment let me down. I felt like Charlie Brown running to kick a football that Lucy would inevitably pull away. I was desperate for some control over my life, be it how I spent my evenings or whom I let into my apartment or how much I weighed. Perhaps these pills could give me back the power to reign over my personal kingdom on all those fronts.

"Are the new pills working?" Sarah asked me as we ate lunch together at work. I blinked a couple times as I tried to form an answer. "Jennette?"

I finally willed my lips to move. "Sorry, I kind of spaced out there."

Sarah continued to stare at me. "Sooooo, are they working?"

I shook my head slowly back and forth, as though I were worried it might topple off my neck if I turned it too quickly. "No, not yet. I feel kind of weird, though."

"No kidding," Sarah retorted. I'd been on Topamax for two or three weeks now, and I was disappointed that it hadn't relieved my pain. "Aren't you hungry?" Sarah asked. She'd been more mindful about food since she started Weight Watchers a month ago. "You've barely touched your sandwich."

I looked down at the peanut butter and banana sandwich on

whole wheat bread. Normally I would have savored every gooey bite of it. Today I'd stopped halfway through, leaving the edge jagged with bite marks in the shape of the European coastline.

"I'm not that hungry," I told her.

As the pills continued to take effect over the following weeks, I didn't notice any change in my headache, but I discovered that they worked fairly well as diet pills. I didn't feel like eating a huge meal in the evenings. I wasn't compelled to raid the fridge for ice cream at nine o'clock. I stopped using binge eating as a coping mechanism for my pain. It was like someone had turned off the crazy switch in my brain that I'd never realized I'd left on.

I'd worked so hard to lose weight, but for the past few months I had been finding that weight again, an ounce at a time. I should have been happy about the U-turn my weight was now taking. Instead, I hated myself for liking it. Diet pills were a lie. They promised you a quick fix to a problem that did not have a quick fix. To lose weight and keep it off, you needed to eat well and exercise, not pop pills. Pills were risky and didn't solve the real problem, which was your lifestyle. Sometimes diet pill retailers asked to purchase advertising space on my blog, but I turned them down because I didn't want to promote their products.

My slow and seemingly uncontrollable weight gain was the maggoty topping on the sewage sundae life had served me, but diet pills weren't going to clear the problems on my plate. Yet here I was, taking medication and losing weight. It was yet another thing I thought I'd never do that I was now doing. I hated how this headache was changing me. Could I even consider myself to be me anymore? If I couldn't rely on my own body to be on my side, I couldn't rely on anything. I should change my name to Janet Foolda; that was the person the nurses called out for.

I also hated that Topamax made me stupid. During one of my research trips into the Internet, I'd found a web site called "Crazy Meds" that explained the side effects of neurological medicines. It was written in plain English by people who had taken the meds. The site told me that Topamax was nicknamed "Stupamax" and "Dopamax." The medication made it harder for me to form sentences, as though someone had placed the English language on the top shelf, just out of my reach. I could see what I wanted to say, but I had to stand on my tippy toes to grab the words, and even then I could only knock them over instead of grabbing them firmly. I was supposed to be the smart girl. It was an indelible part of my identity, and without my brain I didn't know who I was. The crazy switch was turned off, but it had tripped the "stupid" circuit breaker.

At the office, my spacey demeanor continued. I found myself unable to take part in workplace banter. We were always kidding around, but now I found myself unable to make simple connections and form jokes. It was like living life three seconds behind everyone else, as if I were receiving a satellite TV feed from across the planet. I was losing any social capital I had, which was about the only thing I had left at this job. I'd missed several days of work to go to doctor's appointments, and I didn't get much done when I *was* there. Now that my IV was gone, I occasionally wished I would have a seizure in the office. If I fell out of my chair and started shaking violently on the coffee-stained carpet, it would remind them how serious my condition was.

I knew I had to go off the pills, but I tried talking myself into only reducing the dosage. If I went down to 25 mg, I could stay smart but also be thin. *Who need brain?* I thought. *The dumb not so bad. Ouchies worse.* But it was no use. Other people might be fooled about the state of my illness, but I couldn't fool myself.

Food had always been my drug of choice. I'd wanted the pills to work so I could pass off my suppressed appetite as a convenient side effect of the medication. Then I could have told people that I was taking the pills for my headaches, not because they made me thin, although the thinness sure was nice. Not only would my life have been pain-free again, it would have been a little bit easier. I wouldn't have had to battle overeating as much, something I now combated every night in a fight where forks and knives were weapons turned against me.

I followed my doctor's instructions and slowly tapered off the Topamax, glad to reemerge from my zombie state, but sad every time I stepped on the scale. Oddly enough, as my appetite returned, I realized I had missed being hungry. I had missed eating too many ice cream sandwiches at twenty minutes until midnight and feeling pleasantly full. Food was one of life's pleasures, and lately it had been my only pleasure. I'd missed the desire. Wanting food all the time was painful, but not wanting it at all was empty and cold, like the inside of my refrigerator had become.

• • •

"So, Amy says you've lost a lot of weight?" the woman at the bar asked me over the intermittent cacophony of the band onstage. We'd only just met, but we were both here to support my friend Amy, who was playing guitar.

"Yeah, I did," I told her as I grabbed my Diet Coke. I had given up sodas, except when I was at bars. Coke was a welcome alternative to alcohol, which would have turned my headache up a notch like the bassist's amplifier. It didn't have any calories either.

"That's awesome. How much did you lose?"

"Oh, about two hundred pounds," I told her.

"Cool," she nodded, then looked me up and down, which made her pigtails bounce. The silence smacked me in the face.

"I've gained about twenty-five pounds back lately," I told her as if to say *I am aware that I'm chubbier than you would expect*.

"So . . . are you happy with where you are?" she asked.

I paused a moment and replied, "Yeah, pretty much." I contemplated kicking her kneecaps out from under her and was immediately surprised by my uncharacteristically violent thoughts. The closest I'd come to a real fight was the time two brawling kids had smashed into my open locker in middle school, barely missing me as I leaped away. My bagged lunch had not been so fortunate.

I hadn't come here to start a fight. I'd come because I knew it was important to be social and not isolate myself from human beings. I didn't appreciate her implication that I shouldn't be pleased with my body. I *wasn't* very pleased with my body, but for entirely different reasons than what she might think. Any problem with my ass was trumped by the problem in my head.

"I've had a constant headache for over seven months now," I yelled over the noise. "It never goes away."

"You should really see someone about that," she joked. I imagined smashing her face into the bar and driving a broken beer bottle through her eye socket.

"Ha, yeah," I laughed. The imaginary movie playing in my head ended with me, the heroine, breaking a barstool over this woman's back and watching her bloodstained body collapse to the floor. In reality, she took her beer and her boobs to the dance floor, where she rubbed them up against a goth boy. She seemed oblivious to the cruelty she had inflicted.

I walked away from the bar and sat down at a table where my friends were. The secondhand smoke from the bar was aggravating my headache, but this was where the people I knew hung out. For some reason we never went to yoga or the farmers' market together. I was just glad to have friends. I had always been a loner. It was only in the past year that I'd started going out with people and doing things. Even in kindergarten, the teachers had said my socialization skills needed work.

"You want a drink?" Leslie, the drummer's girlfriend, asked as she got up from the table and almost stumbled on her three-inch heels.

"No, thanks," I told her. "It just makes my headache worse."

"Oh, you should take some Excedrin," she said, as she teetered over to the bar.

I stayed at the bar until the last band finished playing at one o'clock in the morning. I went to bed knowing I now owed my body a debt that I would pay for in pain, but hoping the psychological benefit I got from hanging out with my friends would outweigh this cost. Altering my bedtime or sleeping too little or too much was like poking the headache, and now the headache would poke back. Regardless, I didn't want to become a shut-in, so I tried to remain connected to my community of friends in the ways that I could. I'd gone to a movie with my brother a few weeks ago but hadn't had much social contact since then until last night.

As predicted, I spent most of Saturday in bed, occasionally getting up to pee. On Sunday I managed to drag myself to the love seat and stared at the television for fifteen minutes without turning it on. Instead of watching a show, I was entranced by my distorted reflection in the convex black screen. The headache was an unruly schoolchild throwing a tantrum, stomping around so loudly in my head that I was surprised to see that the TV wasn't shaking.

I'd been able to stumble through the motions of my old life for the first few months of this illness, but the constant pain had ground me down millimeter by millimeter every day, like the river that had formed the Grand Canyon. I'd distracted myself with the half-marathon training and the book promotions, but that was all over now, and there was nothing left in its place. All I had was a too-small couch and a cold, quiet living room. While my body might stubbornly stumble forward through time for several more decades, it was becoming clear that my life was effectively over. The first twenty-seven years were great, but I would never be healthy enough to do anything worthwhile again.

I finally turned on the TV and caught an episode of *American*

Gladiators. I watched a contestant swim under a lake of fire and run down a balance beam, dodging large balls aimed at her head. I smiled a little, relieved to know that someone else knew what it felt like for me to struggle out of bed in the morning. When I summoned enough energy to get up from the couch, I thought I saw permanent impressions on the cushions in the shape of my butt.

Despite the effort required, I managed to drag myself out of bed and drive to work on Monday morning. I sat in front of my computer and looked at my tasks, seeing only a list of annoying items to complete. I had lost any interest in my job months ago, which was sad because it was the only thing I had left to do other than attend doctor's appointments. The days had grown shorter because it was autumn, and the Indiana sky was an eternally smoky gray. The familiar pain hummed in the background of my mind. *Hello, my enemy, my old friend*, I thought.

I opened a news site in my browser to distract myself and read about the unveiling of a high-tech atom smasher. Some people were worried that the world would explode when the scientists flipped the switch on. *That sounds good*, I thought. *Then it would finally be over*. Death had always been my worst fear in life, narrowly edging out my fear of the future, which narrowly edged out my fear of a snake crawling up the toilet. I didn't believe in an afterlife, and whenever I started to think about the fact that one day my consciousness would not exist, I felt a cold shower of fear pour over my body. This was the fear skydivers must feel when plummeting toward the ground, unsure if their parachutes will open. It was liquid fear running through my bloodstream, calling itself adrenaline. After only one or two heartbeats, I would become so afraid that I forced myself to think of something else, be it cuddly kittens or calculus formulas or tongue teasers. Death was so scary and undesirable that I could not look at it straight on, as if I were trying to stare at the sun. So it was odd that I was now daring to glance at death, and that when I did, it didn't seem all that bad. Not existing was scary, yes, but existing in pain wasn't that great either.

I busied myself with work, but my mood only got worse as the day dragged on. About an hour after returning from lunch, I stared blankly at my computer screen, then I glanced around the office, searching for something I couldn't see or name. I felt a force compelling me to leave, as if staying one more minute in this room would cause gravity to pin my body to the floor, crushing me beneath the weight of existence. I grabbed my coat and hat from the closet and left the room. I rode down the elevator and walked out the employees' entrance toward the parking garage.

I could leap off the top, I thought.

Just as quickly as the thought came, I dismissed it. Jumping off the roof wouldn't guarantee I'd die. I might end up paralyzed, a burden to my family, with thousands of dollars due in medical bills. No, if I was imagining ways to kill myself, I'd need a different way. Not a gun. That was violent and confrontational in a way I never was. Slitting my wrists didn't sound appealing because I disliked the sight of blood. It would also leave a mess for someone else to clean up. Pills would probably be the best way, but I didn't have access to anything that would do the job. I'd given the leftover Vicodin back to Angela.

I continued this strangely detached line of thought as I walked to my car, not sure if I was serious or not. It would be best if I were caught in a situation like the two motorists who had been killed recently when a semitrailer jackknifed on the highway. No one could blame me for something like that, and my family could collect my small life insurance policy to pay for the funeral.

If I did have to kill myself, would I need to write a suicide note? What should it say? Should I post something on my blog before I did it? What would my readers think? Undoubtedly they would post sad, mournful tributes to me and note what an inspiration I had been and how sad it was that I'd been driven to end my life so early. They would be sad and they barely even knew me.

My family knew me, though. That thought started to bring me back to reality. My suicide would destroy them. If I had a dream that involved my mother or brothers dying, I would awaken with primal fear pumping through my blood. It took hours to evaporate, even though the event wasn't real. I couldn't do that to my family.

Obviously, I'd have to kill them all first and then murder myself.

I rolled my eyes while I climbed the stairwell in the parking garage. This whole line of thought was ridiculous. My brother had a friend who'd leaped off the top of a parking garage, twitching and dying in the street below. He'd stopped traffic for two hours. It wasn't something to joke about. I wasn't seriously considering killing myself, but I couldn't help reviewing my options should the day ever come when I needed to. I was like a woman planning her wedding even though she was not engaged or dating anyone. I was imagining possible scenarios, figuring out the details.

I'd also have to wait several years before seriously considering suicide. I'd read a book recently, called *All in My Head*, by a woman who'd had a headache for decades. If I offed myself after only seven months, I would look like a wimp in comparison. Besides, who would be left to take care of my cats, assuming they didn't eat my dead body first?

I reached my car and unlocked it with my remote button. I crawled into the backseat and slammed the door shut, not really knowing why I'd come out here. I only knew I couldn't stand to stay in the office. I stared blankly through the front windshield at a concrete pillar that had a heart spray-painted on it. The graffiti became blurry as an avalanche of tears ran down my face. The tears kept flowing for so long that I lost count of the minutes. Perhaps the car would fill up with salty water and I would drown myself. My body shook from the sobs, and the car rocked as if two lovers were in the backseat. I let my sadness pour out of me, surprised by how long my bawling lasted. After thirty minutes I ran out of tears.

Feeling dehydrated, I lay back against the fuzzy beige bench, catching a dried piece of Chex Mix in my hair. I hoped no one could see me and that no one had heard me. I wished I couldn't hear my own thoughts either, but there was no insulation from them.

I remained there for another hour. How long would I have to be gone before someone became concerned? It had been ninety minutes. They probably thought I'd just taken a long lunch. I sat back upright, hoping my eyes were no longer red or swollen. The headache and I had a relationship more deeply personal than I had with anyone else. I didn't want my puffy eyes to reveal our intimate encounters to others. I opened the door to my sanctuary and entered the world again. I buttoned up my coat and returned to my desk.

No one had noticed I was gone.

I had lasted through seven months of the headache, and all I could see stretching out before me was another seven months followed by another seven months. It was an endless calendar marked with pain instead of dates, becoming progressively worse every time I flipped the page forward to the next month.

I felt as though I were standing outside of myself, watching depression wreck what was left of my life, like Godzilla attacking Tokyo. I was just a viewer in the movie theater, powerless to stop it, as if the final reel would be the same no matter what I did. Something bad was going to happen to me if I didn't do something.

That night I got on Twitter. For some reason I was always tempted to tell Twitter my darkest secrets, sending them out into the Internet like a message in a bottle. "I am unbearably sad," I wrote in the text box. I hit the enter button, and my note floated out to sea.

Literally one minute later I started getting replies, both on Twitter and on Facebook, where my status was configured to be updated with my latest tweets.

"Are you ok?"—Katybell14

"Unbearably sad? Email me if you need to talk."—Eliza

"Dude, I hear you. Ain't no shame in going on the pills."—Brian

"Mental pain can be just as bad if not worse than physical pain. If you need help, I'm here."—LizzoBee

"What's wrong?"—Fred

I no longer felt only unbearably sad, I also felt unbearably guilty. Now my friends and blog readers were worried about me. I wasn't sure what I had expected when I broadcasted that message on the Internet. Had that been a cry for help? It might have been. I just hadn't expected anyone to notice it for what it was, including myself. I sent out a few quick responses, telling them that I was fine, don't worry, and there was nothing to see here, move along please.

I heard a bing and saw that I had a new email. One of my blog readers had sent me a message that analyzed my emotions over the past few days via my Twitter posts. She said I was having mood swings and should seek professional help. I wasn't sure whether to be grateful for her concern or freaked out by her overanalysis of my tweets.

The readers of my blog seemed to view me as an inspirational figure. I often received comments and emails thanking me for sharing my weight-loss story. These messages frequently credited me for motivating people to pursue a healthier lifestyle. I'd never felt entirely comfortable with this perception. I was happy with all I had achieved, but I figured if someone made a change in their life it was because they wanted to, not because I'd made them. I hated when life resembled a cheesy parable, but all I could do was point people to the right path; they had to walk it themselves.

The reverse was true as well. Wherever I was headed, I'd have to travel there on my own. When I had asked for directions from readers in the form of cures, they'd pointed me in hundreds of different directions. I knew they were trying to help, but it just made things more confusing. My lack of any meaningful progress was making this journey feel a lot less inspirational than the weight-loss journey, which had meandered off the trail itself. My blog hadn't been very cheerful lately, nor had I been posting that much. I wouldn't have been surprised if my more astute readers suspected I wasn't doing well. I didn't feel comfortable talking in-depth about the weight gain on the blog because it inevitably led to talk of the headache, which I couldn't handle right now. I was feeling depressed enough without tempting a reader to comment about how badly I'd let them down.

The next morning I dialed a number I had long since memorized. "And why are you scheduling an appointment today?" the doctor's receptionist asked in her typically irritated voice. She seemed to resent every ill patient who had the audacity to ask to see a doctor.

"I've been depressed. I want to talk to her about going on antidepressants," I said. I hadn't said those words to anyone before. It seemed odd that the faceless voice on the other end of the line was the first one to hear about it. I got an appointment to see my physician the next day.

"How are you feeling?" she asked.

I consciously had to remind myself not to respond to her with a perky "Oh, okay!" as I typically did when answering that question. Acting chirpy and in good cheer was not going to get me Prozac.

"Not so good," I told her in my best depressed voice, slumping my shoulders as I said it.

"So, you've been feeling down lately?" she asked.

"Yeah. I don't feel like doing anything. I had to go cry in the parking garage during work this week." I felt embarrassed admitting that. It sounded pathetic. I decided to tell another story instead. "The other day, I was in line at the grocery in the fast checkout lane when the lady in front of me clearly had more than the maximum twelve items. The clerk at the register told the lady she didn't mind, but the person in line behind her might, so then they both looked at me, and I gave them a look like I was going to smite them with my eyeballs." I tried to reenact the glare at my doctor, but it came off more like squinting.

"The lady in front of me seemed really embarrassed, but the thing is, I hadn't been purposely glaring at her at all. I *wish* I had the energy to be angry. That's just how my face looked, because it's been so hard lately. Going to the grocery makes me feel like I'm running an ultra-marathon." I paused to take a breath, aware that my throat was starting to close up and that my eyes felt wet. Crying might help me get antidepressants, but I was sick of not being able to control my body. I demanded victory on the war against my tear ducts. I would not cry.

"I can't remember what it feels like not to be in pain. I can't remember what it feels like to be happy. I think if I were a dog, they would have put me down by now because no one should live in this much pain." I paused to sniffle. "And I never do well in the winter anyway."

My doctor nodded. "You're not alone in that. A lot of people have started to come in because the lack of sunlight aggravates depression." She scribbled some notes. "Have you had any suicidal thoughts?"

"No," I replied. It was funny how quickly I'd started lying to my doctors. I could barely admit to myself that I'd been thinking so much about death. I couldn't admit it to my doctor.

She wrote a prescription for Celexa, and I started taking the pills, grateful that they were on the four-dollar list at my local pharmacy. The simple act of taking the pills made me feel better, even though it would be two weeks before the medicine could build up in my system and have any real effect. I liked being able to do something about my condition, even if it was as simple as tossing a pill down the back of my throat.

It was either the pills or the placebo effect or the cycle of the moon, but two weeks later I felt okay again. In fact, I felt pretty good. Unlike with Topamax, I didn't mind taking antidepressants. They were so commonly prescribed these days that hardly anyone looked down on them. It was almost chic to compare brands and dosages with friends.

"I feel grrrrrreat!" I told Sarah on instant messenger, imitating Tony the Tiger.

"I'm happy for you," she said.

"It's amazing! It's so nice to feel as though life is worth living again! Wheeeee!!! I love pills!!" I was overreacting and I knew it, but it was nice not to hate the world for existing anymore.

"That's good, Jennette," Sarah replied, with a smiley face at the end. :)

A few weeks later, the manic joy cranked down a notch. My moods mellowed out, and even if I was not dancing in the streets, I no longer felt like flinging myself in front of a car either. My life still sucked, but it seemed worth living again, even if the days ahead were marked with pain. I hoped the atom smasher I'd read about wouldn't make the universe implode after all.

For once, a pill could fix one of my problems.

I heard the four melodic tones of my cell phone chirping from the other room. I rolled over to look at the clock, which burned the numbers 2:18 into my retinas. Two minutes later the phone chirped again, and then again two minutes later. I gently pushed a sleeping cat aside and padded to the other room in my pajamas.

There was a text message waiting from Sarah, my work friend. I waited as the phone loaded the text.

"At the hospital. Suicidal."

There was another message after that one, addressed to me and another one of Sarah's friends.

"You two are my best friends. I love you both."

The first message was two hours old. The last one had come eighty minutes ago. It sounded final.

I stared at my phone again, unsure what to do. Sarah was at the hospital. That meant she was being watched. Had she harmed herself? What was the correct thing to do as a friend? Should I call her? Should I call the hospital? I'd never had a friend try to commit suicide before.

I tried calling Sarah back but got no response. I turned on the computer, looked up the phone number of the hospital, and placed a call. The receptionist wouldn't tell me anything other than to confirm Sarah's presence there. I lay back down in bed, trying to figure out the best plan of action. I got back up and started putting on my clothes. I would drive down there and see how she was doing. If anything happened I didn't want to be the one who had stayed at home in bed.

Just as I was about to step out the door, the phone rang.

"Hiya," drawled Sarah on the other end.

"Hi," I said, shoving as much empathy, understanding, and concern as I could into that one syllable. I'd seen plenty of people do the same thing when talking to me about the headache, so it wasn't hard to do. "Are you okay?"

"Yeah, I'm at the hospital. Sorry to scare you," she said.

"I'm going to come on down and see you, okay?" I told her.

"Oh, that's so nice of you, but really, don't feel any obligation to do that."

"It's not a problem, and I'm already awake. Can I get you anything?" I asked.

She paused for a moment, considering my offer. "Um . . . could you bring me chocolate?" she asked.

"No problem!" I said.

It was a problem.

Chocolate was surprisingly difficult to buy at three o'clock on a Saturday morning. None of the twenty-four-hour grocery stores were on the way to the hospital. I stopped at a twenty-four-hour drugstore instead. It was in a scary part of town where the gas station doors stayed locked at night and you had to do business through a bulletproof window. I bought chocolate and magazines and word puzzles. I am fairly certain I was the only person to buy this combination of items from the store that night.

After driving around the hospital complex for ten minutes, I eventually discovered the parking garage by accident and got the first spot near the door. Evidently the secret to getting good parking was to arrive at four o'clock in the morning. I entered the hospital, passed through several sets of double doors, and found the dimly lit ER. There were fifteen beds lining the walls, divided from each other by curtains. I quickly found Sarah and saw that she was strapped to her bed. There had been days at work when she'd joked about being chained to her desk, but seeing her physically restrained was not humorous at all.

"Hi," she greeted me, raising her arms up in a hug as high as they would go against the restraints. "You brought me chocolate!" she exclaimed.

"Yeah." I placed my bounty on her lap and sat down in a chair next to the bed. Before she could say anything else, I felt the need to confess to her, as if we were both recovering alcoholics who'd bumped into each other at AA. "I've been sort of suicidal myself lately. I had to go out and cry in the parking garage for over an hour a couple weeks ago."

Sarah didn't miss a beat. "Thank God, I'm not the only one!" she exclaimed.

"Seriously?" I said. "You go cry in your car, too?"

"Well, I do it in the bathroom," she said. "I don't usually drive to work."

"Geez, how many people at our office are secretly crying during lunch?"

"I guess working where we do would make anyone suicidal," she said. I sat with Sarah and we talked about our own flavors of sadness as we crunched on M&M's. I thought back on my recent conversations with her and tried to remember her latest tweets. She'd said she'd been having trouble sleeping, and I knew her home life had been a little unsettled lately, but I'd had no idea it had gotten so bad. Even if she'd said something like "I wish I were dead," would I have taken her seriously? I probably would have written it off as a joke about how much the workday sucked. Sarah was always joking.

A woman two beds down from Sarah took a wristband off her arm and threw it past a machine next to the nurses' station. A quiet alarm started beeping from the machine.

"What's that?" I asked.

"Oh, that machine starts beeping if you try to leave the room." Sarah raised her hand up to show me a similar band on her own wrist. "It's a suicide prevention thing."

"Ah, I see." I looked at the stocky woman, who had pouted lips and a stubborn look on her face. She was dressed in a green, polka-dot hospital gown. None of the nurses had noticed the alarm, which made me wonder why they had the device in the first place.

I returned my attention to Sarah, until our conversation was interrupted by an authoritative male voice in the section next to us.

"Okay, Mr. Robinson, you've got some bleeding behind your eye, so we're going to have to drain it." Sarah and I looked at each other in horror, grateful we could not see the procedure taking place behind the curtain.

"I think a bunch of guys are in here because of a bar fight," she said. I looked at a man sitting on another bed who was wearing a leg brace. He had been asked to leave thirty minutes earlier but was still here. There was a banging sound coming from the other suicidal woman's stall. I turned to see her smacking her head against the metal rail of her bed. Her forehead was swelling like an anthill, with beads of blood flowing out of it instead of insects. I had often felt like banging my head against the wall because of my headache, but seeing it done in person made it look far less appealing.

Sarah and I continued to stare at the woman. "Huh," I said. I wasn't sure if I should do something, or if any action I took would be rebuked or possibly put me in danger. This whole situation was well outside of my realm of experience.

A nurse finally noticed the woman banging her head against the rail and approached her. "Becky, what's the problem?" she asked with her hands on her hips.

Becky scooted forward on the bed and then stood up. She walked toward the nurse, then made a sudden dash to the left, grabbing a medical tray and flinging it at the health care worker. The nurse was surprisingly spry, and ducked to avoid the metal platter.

"Becky!" the nurse said. "Call security!" she hollered at the other nurses.

Becky growled as she quickly staggered to the bathroom next

to her bed and locked herself inside. A muted banging came from within. The nurse tried to open the door but failed.

"Security better get here fast," she muttered. "She's going to hurt herself."

Three men dressed in dark uniforms with shiny guns in their holsters and even shinier keys on their belts burst into the room. One of the men fumbled with the keys one at a time, trying to unlock the door, eventually finding the right one. They stormed into the bathroom, and two men pulled Becky out, holding her arms. They walked her to her bed. She resisted, but eventually they succeeded in tying her down.

Another nurse came over to Sarah's area. "We're going to move you," she said. "I don't want you to be too close to that." I hopped up, grabbed my coat, and walked beside Sarah's bed as the nurse rolled her across the room. After she set the brake and left, Sarah and I sat in silence.

"Wow," I finally said.

"Yeah," Sarah responded. After a long, quiet moment, she said, "In the movies, the ER cops don't wear guns in their holsters. That way patients can't grab them and shoot someone." I glanced at the security guards' guns. I glanced around the emergency room. I made note of the cot to my right that I could dive under quickly if necessary.

One of the guards started to leave the room, walking past a woman who was dripping blood on the floor from a cut that hadn't been bandaged properly. We heard him mutter under his breath, "I can't believe the shit that's going down in the emergency room tonight."

"Well," I said to Sarah, "at least this probably isn't normal."

My headache no longer seemed like a big deal. I clearly wasn't the only person in the world in pain. I probably wouldn't even make the list of the top ten most suffering people in this building. A dose of perspective might not be a cure, but it made me feel a lot better about my own situation. No matter how bad your life was, there was always someone whose life was worse.

I ate most of Sarah's chocolate. After she had a psych consult, we went to breakfast together. I dropped her off at her home and checked in with her over the next few weeks. I had known Sarah was having a rough time, but I hadn't understood how bad it had been. I doubted most people realized how close to the edge I had been either. I acted normal at work. I put on a smile. I made jokes and bantered pleasantly. And then I came home and cried so loudly that I scared my cats into the other room.

There was so much suffering in the world that went unnoticed. Now I could see so many things that used to be invisible. I wasn't sure if I should be grateful for that or not.

6

Back Scratch Fever

To: Jennette.Fulda@home

From: Bea@detox

Subject: Possible source of headache

Hi Jeannette,

I occasionally read your blog and I happened to see the one about your headache. I am really sorry to hear about that. There was a time when I did have some pain issues. My husband knows I am really scared of pain and it caused a lot of problems because I went into a depression behind it. Nobody could tell me what the problem was and I felt like the great life I had just disappeared.

Anyway, it turned out that I had an autoimmune problem caused by environmental toxins (mostly heavy metals like aluminum and lead). Anyway, after I did detoxification, I could feel the toxins being pulled out of my head. These toxins cause inflammation (which may be causing your headaches) and when they are brought out from being stored deep in your tissues, the inflammation sometimes gets worse before it goes away. I could feel a burning sensation as the stuff was being pulled out of my brain area.

There are 3 factors that may have caused your headache:

1. Drinking the diet sodas out of aluminum cans. The acid leaches out the aluminum from the can. Also, antiperspirant and cookware can have aluminum, also. I use deodorant from Adidas (you can get it on www.amazon.com)

2. Artificial sweeteners, if concentrated in your tissues (brain) could cause inflammation. You may want to see if other people have had a similar problem from them.

3. Losing so much weight may have dumped even more toxins out into other parts of your body. Many toxins are

stored in fat cells. If you start depleting the fat cells, it's possible that the toxins move to other areas.

The best advice I can give you is to see an alternative healthcare provider. Detoxing on your own can lead to some bad experiences, as I can personally attest to. A hair analysis runs about $100 and can tell you what kind of metal toxins that may be in your system.

I hope this helps. Detoxification of my body has given me so much more energy. I wish you the best.

If you do get relief, I would love to know.

Good luck,
Bea

I wanted a spinal tap. I wanted a stranger to stick a long, thin needle into my spine. I knew it would hurt in ways my headache hadn't yet invented, but I was old friends with my pain by now, and I was willing to meet some of its more prickly relatives. I hoped the results of the test might let me name my disease. I could write "pseudotumor cerebri" on its birth certificate, take some pills, and immediately copy its name onto a companion death certificate. Not having a name for my disease was almost as frustrating as the disease itself. How could I fight something I couldn't name?

Pseudotumor cerebri, also known as idiopathic intracranial

hypertension or benign intracranial hypertension, was the latest disease a blog reader was 100 percent completely sure was the cause of my headache. The condition was a result of unusually high pressure in the spinal fluid, which caused headache and damage to the back of the retinas.

I arrived for my next appointment with Dr. Fairweather, which we had scheduled shortly after the last appointment when he'd prescribed me Topamax. In less time than it had taken me to google my way into a paranoid fugue state, he explained all the reasons why I likely did not have pseudotumor cerebri, such as the fact that an eye exam had shown the pressure in my eyes was normal and that one of the recommended drug treatments for pseudotumor cerebri was Topamax, a drug I had used without experiencing any pain relief. People with pseudotumor cerebri typically felt their headaches worsen when they lay down, whereas my headache's intensity did not vary depending on my position. Dr. Fairweather wanted to try other methods of treatment first, and if we ran out of options, we could do the risky, painful spinal tap later to rule out pseudotumor cerebri.

I pushed back any embarrassment I felt and reminded myself that it was good that I was questioning my doctors and doing research. I had to be my own advocate because no one else was as invested in my good health as I was. This was difficult for me, though. I tended to view doctors as God's representatives here on Earth even though I consciously knew that wasn't true. I had to constantly remind myself that they were as fallible as the rest of us. They definitely held the advantage in the power dynamic, not just because doctors are highly paid and well-educated, but because I was sick and they weren't. Having an invisible disease just made this imbalance worse, since I couldn't prove I was sick, the way a man with a broken arm could. I was always at risk of sounding like a crazy hypochondriac or a high-strung woman who just needed to relax already.

After all these doctor appointments, it was becoming clear that the headache was the disease itself, not the symptom of another problem, such as the brain tumor I had first worried about. Headaches could be either primary or secondary symptoms of disease. If you had a secondary headache, it was a symptom of something else, like pseudotumor cerebri. If you had a primary headache, you had no other underlying condition. Your problem *was* the headache. Approximately 90 percent of headaches are primary.

It was also becoming clear that this headache qualified as a larger disease of some sort, and not the typical, fleeting annoyance that headaches typically are. I was growing to hate the fact that my pain manifested itself as something so common. This made it seem like a trifle to other people, as if it were something easy to treat or just a passing state. I would rather have had an awful pain in my leg that people normally didn't experience, if only so they'd take me more seriously.

I suspected my headache was the result of something wired incorrectly in my brain, just as my "Check Oil" light had been erroneously flashing on my car's dashboard earlier that week. The light had appeared whenever I started my car, even though I'd had my oil changed a week ago. I finally read the manual and discovered I needed to reset a fuse under the hood. Once I did, the light turned itself off. We needed to figure out how to reset a fuse in my brain.

"What about this other thing, New Daily Persistent Headache?" I asked Dr. Fairweather. I thought I had read everything there was to read about headaches, but the combination of search terms I'd entered into Google last week when I was supposed to be working had yielded a new result. The International Headache Society had a set of criteria to classify at least fourteen types of headaches, depending on what side of the head the headache occurred, whether it was constant or intermittent, what increased or decreased the intensity of the headache, and other variables. I had previously thought my headache qualified as Chronic Daily Headache, which "refers to a broad range of headache disorders occurring greater than 15 days a month—in many cases daily—for a period of at least 3 months," according to the International Headache Society. Now I thought New Daily Persistent Headache was a better match.

NDPH was one of the newest headache classifications, and was different from other headaches because most sufferers could pinpoint the exact day the headache had started (for me it was February 17, 2008). They had then experienced chronic headache ever since. I ignored the part of the definition that said victims typically did not have a prior history of headaches because I found it to be very inconvenient. I also paid less attention to the fact that some researchers believed NDPH could be triggered by a viral infection because I only remembered being in good health before my headache. The worst news was that NDPH was one of the most difficult headaches to treat.

I'd printed out the information I'd found on NDPH and presented it to Dr. Fairweather after he'd talked me out of offering up my spinal fluid to him. "Yes, hmm, that's very interesting," he said as he shuffled the pages and quickly ran his left hand through his curly blond hair. "What I'd like to try next is Botox."

"Botox?" I asked.

"We still need to break this endless cycle your headache is trapped in," he said. "Some of my patients have seen great results with Botox. I would inject it into different spots on your scalp, around your forehead, and in your neck, to block the nerve impulses that travel there from your brain. You'd still have full use of your facial expressions, though you might not be able to furrow your brow as well."

"Okay, then, let's do the Botox," I said. If he'd suggested I roll around in whale blubber as a cure, I probably would have asked him, "Sperm whale or beluga?" It had been eight months now and I was running out of medical options. I could be easily convinced to get off at whatever stop was next on this endless sightseeing tour of hell. Botox was typically for the aging and the rich, of which I was neither, but that didn't seem to matter in the world I had entered.

"We'll put together a packet to send to your insurance company which lists all the other treatments we've tried that have failed. This helps justify approval for the treatment. The usage of Botox for headaches is an off-label use of the product." I was annoyed that there were very few medications specifically approved to treat headaches. It made me feel like a guinea pig trying experimental drugs, even if they had been approved by the FDA for other uses. Fortunately, Botox was approved by the FDA as a headache treatment in October 2010, so its use is no longer considered off-label.

"Without insurance, each Botox treatment costs about a thousand dollars." I restrained myself from cursing aloud, but my eyes noticeably widened. "If the first treatment doesn't break the headache cycle, we recommend doing at least two or three treatments." My eyes somehow managed to open even wider. "Some patients see better results after a few months of treatment." I crossed my fingers that my insurance company would approve the procedure. I didn't want to spend what was left of my savings on something that wasn't guaranteed to fix me.

"And if that doesn't work?" I asked. I was starting to make a habit of assuming treatments wouldn't work. Then I was far less disappointed when they failed.

"Well, after that there's not much more that I could try. I could refer you to one of the specialty headache clinics a few hours away from here," he said. I now had one more thing to research when I was supposed to be working.

I left the office and waited for a call from the doctor's office to schedule the Botox treatment. The call never came. The nurse said she would submit the paperwork to the insurance company, but I never heard from them either. I decided to assume that the treatment would be denied if they ever did call me back. Instead, I looked up a clinical trial that was researching the effectiveness of Botox for treating headaches. If I qualified for the trial, I would get Botox for free. I emailed the woman in charge of the study, who told me there would be a 25 percent chance I would be receiving a placebo instead of Botox. And I'd have to travel to Connecticut. Five times. On my own dime. I decided against it.

All this mattered less to me after I did more research about Botox and discovered that some previous studies had concluded it was no more effective than placebo in curing headaches. There were other studies that found the opposite, but at the time the effectiveness of the treatment seemed to be the subject of debate. I wasn't that keen about injecting a paralytic agent into my skull anyway. I remembered seeing a news story about a couple who'd gotten injections contaminated with botulism and were permanently disabled. Such cases were rare, but that didn't stop me from worrying about it.

I also wasn't fond of how quickly Dr. Fairweather had dismissed my questions about New Persistent Daily Headache. I decided it was time to pack up my medical records and move on to the next doctor. I didn't relish the thought of seeking out another doctor, but I knew I had to move on if I was no longer satisfied with my current treatment. I wished doctors really were God's representatives on Earth. I'd be spending a lot less time on Google if they were.

I sat in front of my computer at home and spied the IV pole shoved into the corner. Someone from the infusion pharmacy was supposed to pick it up weeks ago, but I hadn't heard from them either. Now it served as a makeshift hat rack and conversation piece. The light from the monitor pierced the back of my eyes like a toothpick skewering an olive, but I wanted to finish reading emails from my blog readers.

I'd written an entry about my headache, breaking my rule never to blog about it again. My readers had responded by sending me very well-intentioned emails that made me want to murder them.

I knew that most of them simply hated to see me suffer, but their advice typically had no scientific basis or consisted of things I'd already tried. I was starting to doubt that I would ever get better, but I couldn't dismiss the idea that one of my thousands of readers might come up with a legitimate lead. I felt like a homicide detective, searching through hundreds of bogus tips, hoping to find one clue that was legit.

I knew I should be grateful that so many people cared about my well-being, but I couldn't help but be annoyed by the people who sent me information about illnesses that clearly did not fit my symptoms. I felt very sorry for the man with occipital neuralgia, which causes intense stabbing pain on one side of the head, but my pain was bilateral and felt like pressure, not electrical shocks. If I had carpal tunnel syndrome, would a reader try comparing it to her broken wrist? I promptly deleted the email from a reader who suggested I should get a CT scan in case it was a sinus infection. And I wasn't sure why the girl who suggested I had pseudotumor cerebri kept insisting that was what I had. Why should I believe her word over that of both a neurologist and an ophthalmologist who'd actually examined me?

When I got halfway through my emails, I knew the next time someone asked me if they'd discovered what was causing my headache, I was going to reply, "Other people's advice." I knew this would make me sound callous and rude, especially since most people were just trying to help, but I sensed some of them had another agenda, too, like they were trying to win a prize. If they guessed what was wrong with me, they were not going to win a free toaster. They would certainly get my gratitude, but I wasn't willing to give them indentured servitude for the rest of my life.

Several people kept insisting that I had food allergies, either to gluten or to a variety of other foods. I used to weigh almost four hundred pounds, so I doubted I was allergic to food. Still, it would be nice if I could go in for a test and be told, "Stop eating dairy and you'll have your life back!"

I scheduled an appointment with an allergist. The worn vinyl upholstery and wooden wall paneling in Dr. Sacks's waiting room made me think I'd traveled back to the eighties. It didn't help that Michael J. Fox was on the cover of a magazine in the waiting room, making me feel as if I were in *Back to the Future.* I would have preferred to travel into the future, where they might have discovered a cure for what was wrong with me, or at least a way to diagnose it. I picked up the magazine and read the teaser line beneath Michael J. Fox's image, which predictably mentioned how he was bravely fighting Parkinson's disease. I wanted to stab his eyes out with my pharmaceutically branded ballpoint pen. I hated how noble and inspirational Michael J. Fox was. I hated how he always kept a positive attitude. I hated how he still had hope for a cure. I wanted to read an interview with Michael J. Fox about how he hated having tremors every day and how he'd thought about killing himself and how he knew deep down inside that he was doomed to a never-ending life of meaningless pain and suffering.

But I might have been projecting.

"Jennette Fulda?" The nurse called my name, surprising me by pronouncing it correctly. She wore seasonal scrubs that were decorated with witches and jack-o'-lanterns.

I apologized for being ten minutes late to the appointment as the nurse ushered me back to the exam room. She had me blow hard into a device that either measured my lung capacity or was a prop for a practical joke they liked to play on late patients. I watched her take my blood pressure and my pulse and figured I was well enough trained by now to do both for her. Then I sat in the empty examination room to wait for Dr. Sacks.

The tables and chairs in the exam room looked as dated as those in the waiting room. Even the posters on the wall seemed to be yellowing slightly at the edges from age. I sat transfixed by a chart that listed ninety things I didn't know you could be allergic to. A few minutes later, the door flew open and a man in his mid-sixties briskly entered the room, followed by a younger woman.

"Hello, I'm Dr. Sacks," he said, and shook my hand. "This is Dr. Cole. She's doing a rotation here from the med school." I greeted them both, wondering if Dr. Cole was younger than me. It seemed that doctors should always be older than me. How else could I believe that they were smarter than me? Dr. Sacks opened my file and asked, "So what are you here for today?" I knew the answer to this better than my own name. I expertly recited my history, the treatments I'd tried, and the doctors I'd seen, but refrained from commenting on their superior waiting rooms.

"Basically, I know this is a long shot, but it's been eight months now, so I'm exploring all the angles. I've had some friends suggest

I might have allergies and I should get tested for IgE antibodies as well as IgG antibodies, which means a blood test as well as a scratch test, or something." I heard myself speaking and barely understood what I was saying. "I don't know. Just cure me, okay?" I laughed, half-seriously.

Dr. Sacks laughed, with me and hopefully not at me. He held up my CT films to the light and complimented me on my sinuses. "Are your headaches located on one side of the head, or both?" he asked.

"Both." I circled the area of pain on my face with the same motions I would use to apply foundation.

"Have you experienced any numbness, tingling, or paralysis?"

"No," I said, reminded that things could always be worse.

Dr. Sacks continued his queries at a rapid-fire pace, sometimes thinking aloud for the benefit of the younger doctor in the room. He was attacking the problem from all directions, with great focus, as though I'd handed him a Rubik's Cube and dared him to solve it. His queries reflected his knowledge of the circulatory system and the brain and other parts of the body that I didn't necessarily think an allergist would know about. I appreciated the effort and passion he was dedicating to my situation.

After ten minutes of questioning, we had eliminated diseases that made headaches worse in the morning or that caused you to see flashes of light or that were accompanied with nausea. Perhaps sensing the defeat in my voice, Dr. Sacks said, "I haven't given up on you." I smiled out of the corner of my mouth. I wasn't sure if I could say the same about myself.

Dr. Sacks listened to my heart and then nodded to Dr. Cole. "Come take a listen," he said. Dr. Cole pulled her own stethoscope out from under her fair hair and pressed the cold metal circle onto my chest. She paused and listened for about fifteen seconds.

"A murmur?" she said.

"That's what I heard, too," Dr. Sacks replied. "You have a heart murmur."

"Oh my God, so does my cat," I told him. My vet had diagnosed my feline a year ago, so I was familiar with the condition, which was usually benign. "It must be contagious," I joked. All I wanted was a diagnosis for my headache, but I kept getting diagnosed with problems like a venous angioma and a heart murmur. I felt like I'd taken my car to the mechanic for an oil change and been told I needed a brake job, too. "Is this at all related to my headache?"

"Probably not," Dr. Sacks said. "Most heart murmurs are harmless, but I'll order an echocardiogram for you to get it checked out, just in case." I remembered reading about patent foramen ovale (PFO) in one of my various research missions into cyberspace. It's a condition in which a small hole in the heart triggers headaches in people with migraine disease. I couldn't remember the name of the heart condition at the appointment. I asked Dr. Sacks if he'd heard of a hole in the heart causing headaches, but he hadn't.

The doctors left so I could put on an examination gown in private. Then the nurse came in, and I lay facedown on the examination table so she could draw a big black grid on my naked back. She lightly scratched each box in the grid with a different needle, each of which contained a sample of a different food. The nurse shuffled each needle back and forth from the tray to my back to the tray again like an expert blackjack dealer. I wondered if she'd been here since the eighties, too. I lay there for twenty minutes while we waited for my skin to react. The chill from the air-conditioner gave me goose bumps. I kept my head pressed firmly against the flimsy pillow, trying to hear the squishy thuds of my heart murmur.

I heard the door open and had to turn my head awkwardly to see that two nurses had come back into the examination room. One examined each scratch on my back and called out numbers as the other wrote them down. When they were finished taking notes, the first nurse cleaned off my back with rubbing alcohol and I sat up, tying the examination gown around my back.

"So, am I allergic to anything?" I asked her.

"No," she said. I sighed and she chuckled. "Most people aren't upset by that."

I put my shirt back on and waited a few minutes. I killed time by reading allergy handouts that I'd pulled out of a brown plastic bin attached to the wall. The door opened and Dr. Sacks returned with a bag full of medication samples.

"Here's some Singulair that you can try so we can completely eliminate allergies as the cause of the headache," he said. I took the bag and stuck my folded-up handouts inside. "Have you ever tried an organic diet?" he asked.

"No," I said.

"Following an organic diet means that if you can't pull it out of the earth, you don't eat it. No artificial preservatives. No artificial sweeteners. No pesticides or growth hormones. It might be that the twenty-first century is not good for you." I was rather fond of the twenty-first century, with its fine features like voting rights for women and digital MP3 downloads, but I got his point.

"You can eat Amish chicken!" he said spiritedly. I immediately envisioned a chicken wearing a black hat, a jacket, and a shiny belt buckle. I didn't know any Amish people. I wasn't sure where to buy Amish chicken. I wondered if Amish people were allowed to use the Internet to advertise their goods. If not, I was screwed.

"Okay," I said, trying to ride the wave of Dr. Sacks's enthusiasm. His optimism was somewhat contagious, and I was excited about my new heart defect.

"I'm also going to order tests for celiac disease to rule that out, even though you don't have any gastrointestinal symptoms." I knew that if you had celiac disease, your body couldn't tolerate gluten. A friend of mine from high school had been diagnosed with it three years ago, and she frequently bemoaned how much she missed whole-wheat bread. Dr. Sacks finished writing out orders, handed me some more photocopies of articles about allergies and headaches, and walked me to the front desk. The waiting room was now mobbed with people, half of them school-age kids. I looked at my watch and guessed that the children were there getting their allergy shots after school had let out.

I waited patiently in line as Dr. Sacks handed the orders to the head receptionist to be photocopied for their records. The other receptionist was busy shuffling through a stack of messy papers on the desk and talking to the short woman in front of me.

"I'm sorry, Mary. I think those records got sent to the Bentley Road branch. You're going to have to call Chandra over there and then get the approval from insurance."

"That's okay," Dr. Sacks joked from behind the stack of paperwork covering the desk. "Mary knows the system."

I looked at Mary and saw her roll her eyes. "Yeah, I know the system. Been in it for twenty years," she said. I looked at her tired expression, her indifferent shrug of acceptance. Oh yeah, Mary knew the system. I prayed I never would.

My test for celiac disease came back negative. The echocardiogram of my heart revealed no problems either. I did learn that I was getting far less squeamish around doctors. If I was in a public locker room, I would try to change without ever being completely naked. However, when the heart technician had asked me to open the front flap of my gown for the test, I'd practically ripped my shirt open and yelled, "Where do you want me?" My body was starting to become the shared property of doctors and nurses. Partial nudity had become a normal part of my abnormal life. I was also cycling through health professionals so quickly, I doubted I'd see most of these nurses or technicians again, so there was less to be embarrassed about.

I read more about PFO and discovered that the symptoms of headaches triggered by it were different than mine. PFO typically didn't cause constant headaches, just intermittent migraines. Another dead end.

I made my best effort to try the organic diet Dr. Sacks recommended. I used sugar in my coffee instead of Equal, but I was anxious about consuming so many extra calories. The organic fruits at the grocery certainly tasted sweet, but they were also more expensive, hurting my bank account, which was already suffering due to medical bills. When I read the ingredient lists on many of my favorite foods, such as my low-fat yogurt or my Lean Cuisines, I saw that they all used artificial sweeteners or preservatives. I started drinking only water, which meant I was getting up from my desk every other hour to go pee. I couldn't even chew my sugar-free gum anymore.

I lasted three days before ripping open a baby blue packet of artificial sweetener and dumping it into my coffee at work. I'd given it a half-assed try, but I didn't believe artificial ingredients were the cause of my headache. If they were, wouldn't I have always had this problem? I believed some people were allergic to fake sugars, but I didn't think I was one of them.

"Back on the crack?" my co-worker Elliot asked as he grabbed the bottle of honey he kept next to the coffeepot. I tossed the sweetener packets into the trash.

"Yep." I nodded. "Sweet, sweet, fake sugar." I took a delicious, low-calorie sip.

"Have you ever considered someone might have a voodoo doll of you?" he asked. I almost snorted coffee out my nose.

"Ha! No, that's a new one. I give you big props for creativity." I had kept my co-workers informed about the treatments I'd been trying, if only to make conversation about something other than TV and movies, which were the only topics we all had in common. Sometimes I wondered if I would have hidden the headache from them if I'd known it would become a chronic issue, but ultimately

I felt a responsibility to let them know about my disease since it might affect my productivity at work, which would in turn affect their workloads. They demonstrated their support for me and my struggles in the normal office manner—by making fun of it. We frequently made jokes about the age of our boss, Dave's habit of complaining, and Jordan's tendency to giggle when he was uncomfortable. I took the fact that they were joking about my headache to be a good sign. If they were upset about my health, they would have joked about it only when I wasn't in the room, as we often did about the incompetence of the IT staff.

"I thought about buying you some Head On. Apply directly to the head," Elliot joked.

"Oh, I have an even better one," our boss said as he walked into the room holding his morning can of Diet Vanilla Coke Zero. "I bet you have a dead twin living in your brain." Both Elliot and I chuckled.

"That's good, too," I told him. "I think the weirdest theory I've heard is that my headache is being caused by a teratoma of the ovary." They both looked at me, waiting for an explanation. "That's when an egg in your ovaries goes all wonky and starts to grow hair and teeth and other body parts." Both men looked at me in horror. "Sometimes they grow brain cells, too. Your immune system makes antibodies to attack the teratoma because it thinks it's an invading disease. But since the brain cells in the teratoma are the same as your own brain cells, the antibodies attack your brain, too, and you get a headache and go into a coma and then die if they don't figure out what's going on and remove it."

There was a pause.

"I read a *New York Times* article about it," I said.

"Wow, I'm glad I don't have ovaries," my boss said.

I opened the door to my apartment and thought I smelled chicken. My cats brushed against my calves, meowing for food. This behavior made me certain I hadn't left chicken out or else the felines would have devoured it and would have no need to beg. I walked through the kitchen and saw a note taped to my microwave.

Sorry you aren't feeling well. There is a rotisserie chicken in the microwave. I hope you feel better.—Jim

I scrunched up my face, trying not to cry, and ended up just sniffling instead. I was glad I'd given my brother a key to my apartment. I fed the cats, and then took the note off the microwave and stuck it to the fridge with a butterfly magnet to remind myself of his kindness. I took out the chicken to enjoy my dinner. It wasn't Amish, but it was good.

Later that night I started searching the Internet for information on disability insurance. I was growing more and more concerned that I wasn't able to do my job well. There were rumors of layoffs coming up, and I dreaded the idea of being thrown out of the office without health insurance or a means to pay for COBRA. Of course, that might be a good thing if the headache was environmental and went away after I no longer worked in that building. I doubted it, though, because I'd been away for up to five days at a time during my book promotions and the headache had never relented.

After reading several boring tomes about disability, I learned I likely wouldn't qualify for it because I was not disabled enough. I had to be incapable of earning any income, which wasn't the case since I was still able to barely hold down my job. I was also capable of working a retail job or waiting tables if I had to, though I was fairly certain those jobs would be miserable in ways that had nothing to do with my headache.

Now that the lead on allergies had dried up, I wasn't sure where to go next. Last month I'd seen the eye doctor, who had charged me $100 to tell me I didn't have eyestrain. When I'd gone for my dental checkup before that, the dentist had cleared me of temporomandibular joint disorder (TMJ). He'd also made me an expensive mouth guard to wear at night in case I was grinding my teeth, but that hadn't done anything either, except save my molars some trouble.

I trudged into work the next day and found myself staring at the computer monitor, unsure of what to google next.

"Ugh," my co-worker Dave said as he leaned back in his chair. "I've got a mean headache." Whenever people mentioned the word "headache" lately, I would react as if they had said my name. I looked up and then glowered at Dave as he rubbed his temples. He stopped suddenly, as if the force of my glare had physically slapped him.

"Uh, sorry," he said and sat up straight again. "I shouldn't complain," he apologized and then pretended to type something.

I stopped glaring and opened my desk drawer instead. "I've got Tylenol and ibuprofen," I told him as I took out the bottles. "If that doesn't work, we can move on to the good stuff I keep in my purse."

He got up from his desk and took the bottle of Tylenol. "Thanks," he said before dry-swallowing the pills.

"No problem," I told him, placing the bottle back in my drawer, which lately resembled a small pharmacy. "And don't worry. I'm sure your headache will go away." Thirty minutes later Dave was typing happily at his desk.

As always, my headache remained.

7

Stick a Needle in Me

To: Jennette.Fulda@home

From: Carlos@ShoutItOut

Subject: PAIN HEALER

I WOULD LIKE TO INTRODUCE MYSELF AS A PAIN HEALER

TILL DATE I HAVE HEALED ABOUT 14LAKHS OF PERSONS FROM THEIRPAINS WITH JUST TOUCHING PLACE OF PAIN BY ME. {WITHIN A MINUTE THE PAIN VANISHES IMMEDIATELY} I HAVE VISITED UPTILL MORE THAN

12 COUNTRIES AND WHEREEVER I VISITED THEIR HUNDERED OF PEOPLE CAME FOR RELIEF OF THEIR PAIN

I HAVE CURED SCIATICA,MIGRAINE,ASTHMA, TUMERCANCER,PARKINSON ELEPHANTIASIS, AND ALL JOINT PAINS. HEADCHES,SINUS PAINS, SPONDYLITIS,NECK PAINS,ALL KINDS OF BODY PAINS,ETC,. ONCE I CURE THE PAIN FROM A PARTICULAR REGION IT SELDOM IF ITS EVER EFFECTS THE SAME AREA AGAIN.

To: Jennette.Fulda@home
From: Clara@Psychic
Subject: This might help

I had headaches for 6 months non-stop and found out they came from tomatoes and corn, which I am not allergic to, they just give me (migraines if I let them get bad) headaches. No corn and tomatoes, no headaches. Some chips and salsa- three days of headaches. It's pretty simple. I figured out the cause of my headaches by calling a medical intuitive (psychic) and this woman, over the phone, who never even saw me told me what my problem is. I sound like I'm crazy right? Maybe an easily influenced hypochondriac? Could be, but if you want her phone number drop me an email. I'm headache free.

As I lay on my chest with needles sticking out of my shoulders, the Chinese lady said, "I'm going to hook these up to electricity, okay?"

I tried to nod, but couldn't because my face was held snugly in the massage table's headrest, so instead I said, "Okay, yeah, sure."

I had just met this woman. She spoke with a thick accent I only 88 percent understood. Yet I was letting her send electricity through needles stuck into my back. Not only that, I was paying her to do it.

The previous Thursday I had been doing research at my computer, with the television playing in the background. It had been nine months since the start of my headache, which meant there was a woman in the world somewhere who had gotten pregnant on February 17, the day my headache began, and now had a baby, as well as tons of free baby shower gifts. It would be fun to throw a shower for my headache, where I could receive lovely items like massage lotion, stress balls, and noise-dampening headphones.

I'd been to all the traditional doctors listed in my health care directory, so now it was time to take a detour into alternative healing. I looked oddly at people who talked about disruptions in my energy flow, but I didn't have much left to explore. There were dozens of items remaining on my imaginary checklist titled "Things that probably won't cure the headache, that I will spend thousands of dollars on anyway just to make sure."

I was only half-listening to the deep, comforting tone of the newscaster when he started to say something that made me turn away from my monitor. The station was doing a story about the benefits of acupuncture for breast cancer patients. I watched the footage of a woman with needles stuck in her body and was surprised by how relaxed she looked. *Okay, I guess I'll get some needles jabbed into my head already.* Although I was skeptical about many alternative healing practices, I knew acupuncture had been proven more effective than placebo in several medical studies. I was willing to accept that there was a lot we didn't know about the human body, and some treatments might work for reasons we did not understand. It seemed worth a try.

I checked my health care policy and discovered it did not cover acupuncture. Since I'd be stuck with the bill regardless, I could choose any practitioner I wanted. Unexpectedly, being responsible for the choice stressed me out. How was I supposed to find a qualified acupuncturist who wouldn't stick me with rusty nails? How could I figure out who was a competent professional and who was using leftovers from their sewing kit?

I asked my friends for recommendations. They were of no help. No one had an acupuncturist in their cell phone's address book. As always, I turned to the Internet, my *real* friend. I browsed several local practitioners' web pages. I knew it wouldn't be wise, but I wanted to pick the person with the best web site design. I found a site listing licensed acupuncturists in my city and finally settled upon a woman who had several certifications. I would go to her and hope she didn't kill me, but if she did I hoped she would do it quickly so I could stop being in pain all the time.

The acupuncturist's office was located in a small office park with nicely trimmed hedges and a small fountain. I walked into the cozy lobby and took off my hat and scarf to see that it resembled any other doctor's office. There were educational degrees hung on the wall next to framed copies of news articles she'd been featured in. I saw pamphlets in the corner that contained more information about acupuncture and other pain treatments, such as massage. There was a small space for the receptionist behind a counter that was separated from the room by a sliding Plexiglas window.

Summoned by the electronic chime of the door, a short Asian woman entered the lobby and welcomed me with a wide smile. I was surprised that she wore a white doctor's coat. I wasn't sure if she was actually a doctor in the Western sense of the word, but the attire subconsciously reassured me about her abilities. Costuming was everything. I didn't know what I had expected, but the atmosphere of this place was very mundane. There were no Chinese decorations on the wall, no incense burning, and no Asian music on the sound system. The office was just quiet and cold.

"I need you fill out forms," Dr. Chang said as she handed me a clipboard with several sheets of paper. I sighed and sat down as she disappeared through the door from which she'd entered, presumably to tend to another patient. I'd been filled with unexpected joy when I'd made this appointment because all the doctor had asked for was my name, phone number, and what time I wanted an appointment. When I had called the allergist, I'd had to give my birth date, health insurance information, social security number, home phone number, cell phone number, work phone number, and emergency contact information. They'd gotten everything but my jeans size.

If hell existed, it consisted of me, sitting in the lobby of a medical office, filling out 500 pages of forms with the same questions on every page. I wasn't sure how my maternal grandmother's diabetes figured into my illness, but I had to make sure to jot it down. I was now an expert at circling the area on the illustration of the human body where I had pain, like a child doodling in a coloring book. I knew other countries used electronic medical records to eliminate repetitive paperwork like this, and I wished the United States would become one of them.

Dr. Chang returned a minute after I'd finished filling out the forms. "Do you need to use restroom?" she asked. I told her I was fine, and we went back into one of the three treatment rooms. It looked like any doctor's office. There were sterile white sheets on the table, medical waste containers in the corner, and charts on the walls. Lines connected circles and stars on the chart like a pattern sketched by a Spirograph. They also had notations about the liver and spleen and kidneys. There were illustrations of the hands, feet, and other body parts, with red dots demonstrating where a needle should be inserted. The title referred to something called "The Five Elements Law."

I sat down in a chair next to her desk as she reviewed my forms. "So where your pain?" she asked. I talked about my pain once again. I tried to describe it consistently at each doctor's office. I didn't want to be a police suspect who kept changing her story. Words like "tightening" and "pressure" didn't fully express the agony that had been haunting me lately. I wanted to hook her brain into my body for a moment, so she could feel what I felt, so she could truly understand how I hurt.

"I've had a headache for over nine months now," I told her.

She winced like I had pinched her. "Oh, so, so sorry," she said genuinely, as if we actually had been hooked into each other's nervous systems. I smiled ever so slightly while she made some notes. She had earned her $70 in just that half-second. There was no need to stick me with needles. Her empathy had made me feel validated. I had a witness to my pain, someone who acknowledged that it was real and that it was a true burden.

This was one of the advantages an alternative health worker had over traditional doctors. My acupuncturist was not overburdened with patients like the majority of the medical system was, so she could spend more time with me instead of rushing off to take care of the next person. She could sit and listen and empathize, which was something I craved almost as much as relief. My acupuncturist had just made me feel human, and not like another insurance claim to be filed at the end of the day.

We reviewed the rest of my symptoms and the pills and vitamins I was taking. I mentioned that my neck had been hurting lately as well. Then she got up, handed me a gown, and left the room as I changed. When she returned, I was lying facedown on the table as I had been instructed to do.

I heard Dr. Chang walk up beside me. Warm hands pressed on a spot on my shoulder. "This where pain is?" she asked.

"Yes," I replied. A moment later, I flinched at what I presumed was an incredibly fine needle swiftly entering that spot of flesh.

"You feel that?" she asked.

"Yes," I definitely felt that. It stung for a second, but then the pain faded as quickly as it had begun. The needle was so thin that it didn't hurt like the IV starter needle had, though I could still sense the metal's presence in my body.

She proceeded to feel more spots on my shoulder, asking if I felt chronic pain there. If I said "no," she'd press the needle slightly deeper and ask me again if I felt that. A "yes" was followed by a new staccato tap from another needle. She inserted almost twenty needles into my back. Then I felt movement as she clipped some wires onto the needles, connecting them to a box on a table.

"Tell me when it starts to vibrate," she said as she turned a knob I could not see. Electricity started to flow from the device into my body. I hoped that the machine was plugged into a surge protector.

"I don't feel any—oh, okay, yeah!" I said as the needles started to vibrate pleasantly on my right side. Then she repeated the procedure on the left shoulder.

"You cold?" I was, so she turned on a space heater on the floor near my feet. I felt waves of heat emanating from the metallic cone at the back of the device. "Want music?" she asked.

"Sure," I replied. She turned on the boom box, which played the calming sound of piano and violins.

"Okay, I be back in fifteen minutes," she said and then left the room. Leaving me alone. With needles in my back. Plugged into an electric socket. Listening to Muzak. Which left me plenty of time to wonder how I'd gotten myself into this situation.

It was a bit late to do anything about it now. I had technically chosen to come here, but I didn't feel like there had been much choice. What other options did I have? Should I have stayed home instead, mindlessly watching *Grey's Anatomy* in the hope of a clue?

The lights were dimmed, which I guessed was supposed to help me relax. I tried to let my consciousness float adrift. I couldn't quite turn my mind off, but it was nice to take time out, lie down, and let life pass by for several moments unhindered by a desire to be productive.

Dr. Chang soon returned to unclip the wires and remove the needles from my back, dropping them into a red hazardous waste box. I then flipped over and closed my eyes as she felt areas on my face.

"Hurt here?" she asked. She tapped needles into my face, around my temples, and into part of my scalp. She left the electrodes on the table this time. Once she left the room, I closed my eyes and retreated back into my body. The needles around my temples started to hurt while she was away. When she came back thirty minutes later she asked, "Is headache gone?"

"Sorry, no." I felt basically the same, though slightly buzzed or dizzy. I wanted to tell her, "Yes! You have cured me!" and offer my credit card up to her in thanks, but it would have been a lie. I hated letting her down. I was a people pleaser who'd tried to quit the habit, but I still found myself fighting the urge to make other people happy, even at my own expense. She wanted me to get better and I wanted to get better for her, but it hadn't happened.

I scheduled another appointment, though I doubted it was worthwhile. I had started to view my medical appointments as work I had to do to earn my "piss-off policy" for that treatment. It was like earning patches for my sash when I had been a Girl Scout. I would go to the acupuncturist, give it a good try, and then when it didn't work I could tell everyone who suggested acupuncture to piss off. I was also the kind of person who read to the end of a bad book just so I could tell people that I really did hate the whole thing. The piss-off policy cost money and time, but it would be worth it so I could tell people to piss off without remorse.

I returned a week later during lunchtime on the one day of the week I was allowed to work from home. "You need to use rest-room?" she asked again as she must do before every treatment. She was nothing if not consistent. Disease had made my life very repetitive. I always seemed to be sitting in waiting rooms or answering the same questions over and over again.

I told Dr. Chang that my neck felt better, so this time I didn't have to put on a gown. Instead she had me lie on my back with my jeans rolled up to my knees. She inserted the long, thin, metal pins into a few points on my feet, knees, and hands as well as in my face.

After she left, I tensed my brow for a few seconds and felt a drizzle of endorphins flowing through my face around the area where the needles were. I tensed the muscles again and released them. I felt a gentle tickle around my nose. I wasn't sure if tensing my face muscles like this was helping, but it felt good in an odd way.

Dr. Chang let me percolate for forty-five minutes before returning. "How is headache?" she asked.

"Hmmm, it's still there, but I feel pretty good," I told her. It was like I'd taken a Vicodin without self-medicating. I floated out to the lobby, where Dr. Chang sold me a bottle of herbal supplement pills.

"This help sinus," she said.

"Okay," I said with a smile as I happily handed her my credit card.

The buzz lasted for several hours, but eventually I floated back down to Earth like a skydiver with a parachute. I wanted to get back in the airplane to make another jump, so I came back again a week later and enjoyed a similarly pleasing experience.

The next three times, I felt nothing. Rather, I felt the needles puncturing my skin and the cool moisture of the alcohol swabs as she prepared the area, but the happy, fun endorphin high was not flowing through my body. On each subsequent visit, Dr. Chang seemed more and more disappointed when I answered her question "Still have headache?" I'd given this a decent try, and it hadn't been 100 percent unsuccessful, but after six visits I decided to let her and my bank account off the hook.

"Let me try one more thing," Dr. Chang said after my final treatment. She left the room and quickly returned with a package of small metal balls that were each attached to individual pieces of sticky tape. She attached three balls on the front of one ear and then stuck three more in the same places on the back of the ear. She did this on the other ear, too. Dr. Chang told me to squeeze them twenty times when I had a headache.

We walked to the lobby, where I paid her. "When you want next appointment?" Dr. Chang asked. I started to feel tense. I hated breaking up with doctors. I was a coward and wished I could do this over the phone or via email instead. I'd never told my last neurologist that I was leaving him, and thankfully he hadn't seemed to notice.

"Well, I think this will be my last one," I told her. "My insurance doesn't cover this, and I can't afford to come anymore. Thank you, though, for all that you've done." It was easier to blame the money, which wasn't a total lie. I omitted the part about how she'd failed to cure me, though I'd never really thought she would. I no longer expected someone to wave a magic wand over my body and heal me instantly, as I had back in February. I did believe that my practitioners wanted to do their jobs well. They wanted to make me better. The longer I stuck around, the longer they would feel like failures who were bad at their jobs. I didn't want that, either for them or for myself.

I walked out to my car and sat for a moment. The metal balls had quickly cooled in the winter air. I gave them a squeeze and then flipped down the overhead mirror to look at myself. I looked like I was wearing hipster jewelry.

I drove off into traffic, knowing the way home, but not knowing where to go after that.

I came home to my empty apartment. The dirty dishes in my sink had now piled up so high on the counter that I couldn't open the microwave door. The living room was cluttered with books, DVD cases, and other detritus of modern life. I'd never let it get this disorganized before. The state of my apartment was usually a reflection of the state of my mind, and we were both a mess lately. I needed to devote my energy to seeking treatments and trying to work, so I'd set lower standards in other areas of my life, like cleanliness.

I used to exercise after work by running on the trail near my apartment. I knew exercising would increase my overall health and generate some happy, post-workout endorphins, but I didn't have the energy to give a damn about it lately. Of course, if I'd had the energy, I wouldn't feel as bad about not exercising. This was a self-perpetuating tailspin I couldn't pull myself out of. I looked at all the blank boxes on my calendar where I used to write down information about the workouts I had completed. All I saw on my calendar now was a note about a pain seminar that was being held downtown at a university that night.

I drove to the lecture hall where a doctor who specialized in pain treatments was speaking. I took the escalator up to the third floor and walked into the room. I immediately categorized everyone who was sitting at the five rows of tables into two groups: bright young medical students and old people in pain. I could have been wrong, since I myself was a young person in pain, but I felt heartened that others in this room might have thought about piercing their eyes out with a pair of scissors today, too.

I'd found my people.

A projector displayed a slide on the wall that said, "Myths and Facts of Pain: Is it all in your head?" I found the title ironic, because whether my pain was all in my head or not, it was definitely in my head. If given the choice, I would have transferred the pain from my head to my leg or my arm, because it seemed that would be easier to bear. There was something about having the pain in my skull, the place where my consciousness lived and worked and played, that made it particularly distracting. I could see myself living without a hand or a foot, but I couldn't live without my head.

I grabbed some carrot sticks from the free food table, ignoring the brownies in a small, though probably futile, attempt to prevent more weight gain. I sat down and set up my digital MP3 player to record the lecture.

A tall man wearing a crisp white shirt and dress pants addressed us from the front of the room. "Hi, everybody. I'm Dr. Mason, a professor of Clinical Medicine in the Department of Internal Medicine. I treat patients with persistent pain. Just to start us off, let's see a show of hands. How many of you have been in constant pain"—I put down my carrot stick and began to raise my hand—"for more than ten years?" I quickly put my hand down and then turned around.

Nine people had their hands up. My heart hurt for them, and so did my head.

One man who had raised his hand also had a cane leaning next to his seat. A year ago when I had seen a man walking slowly with a cane in front of me, I had thought, "I wish he'd walk faster." Now if I saw the same man, I'd probably still wish he would walk faster, but I would also think, "He must be in a lot of pain," and I would forgive him for any inconvenience his slow pace caused me. We were now comrades.

Most of Dr. Mason's lecture went flying over my head and splat into the wall behind me, but the parts I did understand were depressing. Due to a concept called "neuroplasticity," meaning the brain's ability to change, the longer you were in chronic pain, the more likely you were to remain in pain. This constant state of suffering caused physical changes in your brain over time that effectively taught your body to stay in pain. Chronic pain could also make portions of your brain shrink over time, which was ironic since I constantly felt like my brain was too big for my skull.

Dr. Mason had more bad news for me. Women had fewer receptors in their brains that bind to morphine, which was what made you feel less pain. Also, the response level of these receptors varied during the menstrual cycle, making your body's ability to gobble up feel-good morphine vary depending on the time of the month. This explained why my headache would often get worse once a month.

"Now I'm going to talk about pain versus suffering," Dr. Mason said. "Even if you are constantly in pain, how much you suffer from the pain depends on your emotional state, your attitude, and your environment. It also depends on your ACC, the anterior cingulate cortex, a portion of your brain that lights up to tell you to pay attention to the pain." I felt like my headache had gotten worse just by listening to this lecture, backing up Dr. Mason's statement that suffering was worse when you paid attention to your pain. If all I was doing was thinking about my headache, I couldn't help but seem to suffer more from it. The headache seemed less painful if I distracted myself from it with a task that required focus and concentration, like writing or playing a video game. The pain became like a bad song on the radio that I'd unwittingly listened to for a minute, distracted by traffic, before realizing it was playing.

After having this thought, I noticed that I had tuned out of Dr. Mason's talk for a minute, too, listening to myself think instead of to the doctor talk. I was intrigued by the idea of pain versus suffering. It seemed that even if I couldn't control the level of pain I was in, I could modulate the amount I suffered from it. Pain was a perception created in the brain, and that perception could be distorted, if not eliminated. Acupuncture had worked that way the two times it had worked at all. I'd gotten a buzz that made me feel better for a few hours even if it hadn't healed my head. My binge eating made me feel better, too, but it was a destructive habit. I needed to find healthier alternatives. Yet I was still pissed off that I had to find alternatives at all. I didn't want to change my life because of the headache. I wanted my old life back.

After an hour, Dr. Mason's talk concluded. As I drove home, I heard a bad song playing on the radio. I sat at a stoplight, trying to tune out the music instead of turning it off, but before the light turned green, I reached out and changed the channel instead.

8

Adjustments

To: Jennette.Fulda@home

From: Katie@SpaceCase

Subject: Saw this and thought of you

Hey Jennette,

I read an article on a news website recently and thought of you. They said microgravity has caused two-thirds of 17 astronauts to get headaches when they are in space, but they are pain free on earth. Have you been on any spacewalks recently?

To: Jennette.Fulda@home

From: Eva@wireless

Subject: Thought you should know this . . .

I was reading a magazine the other day with an article about some guy who had a debilitation headache like yours. He worked on the computer a lot, and his wife noticed that his headache started when they installed a wireless internet router. They turned it off, went back to hardwired Internet and his headaches went away.

Since you're a web designer, I wanted you to know about this.

Good luck.
No need for any response.

I didn't have high hopes for the chiropractor, but I felt the need to keep doing something, anything, to attack the problem that was attacking me. My family had done the same thing in their own way. My brother had brought me a chicken dinner, and my mom had dropped by a few times to do my dishes. I knew those tasks made them feel better since it allowed them to take action. It also helped numb the fact that they couldn't do anything to cure me (except complete degrees in neuroscience). I doubted that the chiropractor could make me better, but at least I was still fighting this headache in every way I could. I hadn't laid down my arms on the battlefield yet.

However, I was starting to think the scariest thought of all: There was nothing I could do. There was nothing anyone could do. I think my friends and family were beginning to suspect this as well. They wished and prayed for me to get better because they hated to see me suffer, but I think they also did it because the idea that there was no cure scared them. If a healthy, young woman like me could be struck down by disabling pain, anyone could. We lived our lives in happy denial of the worst possibilities. Every time I got in a car, I bet I would not die in an accident, but every day someone else thinking the same thing was left a lifeless corpse at a crash site. Shit happens, sometimes for no reason at all.

This fear might also be why my blog readers kept sending me potential cures. They wanted to make order out of the chaos. They wanted there to be a reason I suffered as I did. The human mind was designed to find patterns, which was why a cloud might look like the shape of a bunny rabbit. This was why they came up with such cockeyed explanations for my headache. It was scary to accept that there might not be a reason, or if there was one, I would not know it in my lifetime. It was easier to blame Splenda.

"I'll need to see your insurance card, just as at any good doctor's office," the receptionist at the chiropractor's office said as she stared at her computer. In turn, I stared at her freckled face and wondered why she felt the need to say "good doctor's office." At all the good doctor's offices I'd been to, they never felt the need to recite their accreditations while I signed in. The phrase had probably been meant to set me at ease, but it made me feel apprehensive instead, as if she were overcompensating for something.

I sat down in the lobby to fill out yet another set of forms. There was a Christmas tree twinkling in the corner of the waiting room. I looked at the presents sitting on the green felt tree skirt and hoped Santa had brought a cure wrapped in a box. I turned in the forms and was guided to a warm, muggy examination room. It was a stark contrast to the cold December winter outside, so much so that I began to sweat under my long-sleeved shirt. I waited for the doctor to come in. I was getting very good at waiting.

"Hello, I'm Dr. Jonas," a tall man said as he closed the door. He'd almost had to bend down to avoid knocking his head on the door frame. He wasn't wearing a white doctor's coat, which was a wardrobe change from the other health practitioners I'd been hanging out with lately. Instead he wore dress pants and a button-down shirt.

"So tell me about your problem," he said in a relaxed Midwestern drawl. I wished I had a prerecorded videotape I could play that recited my symptoms instead of having to recount them again and again. The chiropractor was engaged, making eye contact with me and asking questions as I stated my symptoms. Then he asked me to hop onto the table, and I heard a familiar crunching sound as my butt made small creases in the sterile white paper.

"Turn your head as far as you can to the left," he said as he pulled out a clear plastic protractor that would measure how much rotation I had in my neck. Dr. Jonas held it up next to my face and wrote down a number. I turned my head this way and that. Then he pushed down on the top of my head. We did other tests in which I held my arms or legs out and he tried to push and pull my appendages toward him or away from him, seeing how strongly I could resist. He interwove his fingers with mine and I squeezed as hard as I could as he pulled his hand away from me. It was similar to the neurological exam I'd had, but this time I half-expected him to start a playground clapping game with me as we sang "Miss Mary Mack."

"Your right shoulder slumps a bit," he told me. There was no mirror in the room, but when I went home later that night I could see that it was true, though I'd never noticed it before. People always said I had a tendency to slouch, which I noticed only when I looked at photos of myself.

"Here's what I'd like to do," the chiropractor continued. "I want to take some x-rays to look at your neck before we do any adjustments." He grabbed a life-size model of the human spine from the corner of the room. The vertebrae were made of white plastic, and there were yellow cords of nerve fibers sprouting out between the bones. It reminded me of a technique in the *Mortal Kombat* video game in which a character delivers a killing blow by ripping out the victim's spine. I briefly mulled the idea of finding a ninja to try the technique on me.

"Headaches can sometimes be caused by irritation of the nerves in the cervical section of the spine up here," he said as he pointed to the top curve of the model near the base of the neck. The name "cervical" confused me because the last time someone had taken a look at my cervix, they'd also gotten a good look at my lady bits. I let it go and continued to listen. "After we look at the x-rays, I can determine a course of treatment to possibly loosen the tightness in your neck and ease the irritation." He also spouted lots of medical mumbo jumbo that my brain understood as well as it did a Japanese cartoon.

"Okay," I said. "Let's do that." I was the most agreeable patient in the world. I wondered how weird a treatment would have to be before I'd actually object to it.

We took the x-rays, and I came back a few days later for my follow-up appointment. I was ushered into a large room that was divided in half by a hanging curtain. My side contained two chairs, a TV, and a light box on the wall used to examine x-rays. The other side of the curtain contained a chiropractor's table and a device that looked as though it was designed to transport Hannibal Lecter.

"I'm going to pop in a video for you to watch that explains some basics. When it's done, give me a holler," the freckled receptionist said before she left the room.

I watched the video, which I could tell was produced in the eighties because of the cheap onscreen graphics and the fact that it was on tape, not DVD. It talked about subluxations and life energy and other topics I'd never heard of before. The fact that this information had never been covered in science class made me nervous. I was a fairly skeptical person, and I knew I'd need to read a few peer-reviewed journal articles about subluxations before I believed they were real.

On weight-loss blogs, I frequently saw ads for acai berries, hoodia, and other treatments that seemed more like snake oil than long-term solutions to a weight problem. I assumed there were similar products in the world of chronic pain, but I wasn't as experienced in spotting them. I hadn't made up my mind about chiropractic treatment yet, but I'd had mixed feelings from the start. One friend had told me that the only thing that cured her back pain was a visit to her chiropractor. Another friend warned me that all chiropractors were quacks. I had only gone to the chiropractor because I didn't have any other place left to go in town. This video was meant to educate me, but it was only making my confidence in the profession drop.

I wanted to be open-minded toward treatments that might help me, but I didn't want to be taken advantage of either. There were many things about the human body that we didn't know, a fact proven by the reality that no one could figure out what was wrong with me. There seemed to be no absolute truths in medicine. Everyone had a different opinion about what could be wrong and what treatment I should follow, but the video's vague talk about "life energy" was making me second-guess my decision to come here.

The tape wasn't half over before I had the urge to sneak out of the room, crawl past the reception desk, and get into my car to drive as far away as possible. After the video ended, I stared at the black television screen for several moments, wishing I'd gotten to watch one of the kids' videos lying under the TV stand instead. I looked at my watch, wondering how late I'd be to work because of this appointment. Yesterday afternoon my boss had sent me an email filled with slightly restrained anger because I hadn't completed the mock-ups for a web site that were due. I had tried not to cry when I responded to his email and apologized. I had wanted to finish the work on time, but I hadn't been able to push through the pain that day to get anything done. I had vowed to complete the work this morning as soon as possible.

THUMP!

I heard a loud sound coming from down the hallway. Ten seconds later I heard it again. THUMP! I started seriously considering that escape plan.

After I'd waited for ten minutes, Dr. Jonas walked in with my x-ray films. "Thanks for waiting," he said. I refrained from telling him about my plan to crawl out the front door. He clipped my films to the light box on the wall and flipped the switch on. "You have scoliosis," he said. I looked up at the x-ray and saw that he had drawn a straight line down the image of my spine with a pencil. Indeed there was a slight curve, though nothing close to a dramatic "S" shape.

"Whoa, for real?" I asked, suddenly captivated by the films. "They tested me for that in middle school and never said anything about it."

"Unfortunately, most cases are not caught with the simple test where you bend over to have your back examined." Dr. Jonas said scoliosis could also be detected by looking at a person's posture and the way they held their body. "You also have a forward neck curve," he said as he pulled up another x-ray. "It's probably caused by all the computer work you do." Dr. Jonas took out a number-two pencil, a ruler, and a protractor to draw lines on my x-rays. He talked about the angle at which my spine was supposed to curve and how mine was outside of the recommended parameters. He made the films sparkle with shiny graphite. I was dazzled.

The skeptical part of my brain wondered if this was all bullshit, but if it was, it was definitely my brand of bullshit. I loved algebra and geometry and word problems that involved rotating lighthouses. I had been hesitant to visit alternative health practitioners because I didn't believe they had the science to back up their methods. But Dr. Jonas enthralled me with a protractor and precalculus. He reminded me of sine and cosine and complementary angles, all of which were things I believed in and knew to be true. He would cure me . . . with math!

"So, what do we do?" I asked. He recommended an initial aggressive treatment plan of three adjustments a week for the first two months. Then it would be dialed back to two adjustments a week, then less and less.

"What is your insurance coverage like?" he asked.

"I have a forty-dollar co-pay and it covers twenty-five visits a year," I told him.

"Okay, you won't run over that in the next two months," he said. Any trust we'd developed over our shared love of complementary angles was now dissipating. Was Dr. Jonas looking out for me and my ability to afford his services, or was he determining how much he could make off my treatment? Both? I wasn't sure.

I scheduled my appointments and later told everyone I knew that I had scoliosis. I'd wanted someone to find out what was wrong with me for so long that I was ecstatic to have a spinal deformity. Every other doctor had told me I was in practically perfect health, and I was probably the only person in the world to be disappointed to be considered so well. Scoliosis was something real, solid, and visible on an x-ray. I preferred it enormously to my invisible disease. Also, the next time someone told me I had poor posture, I would be able to tell them they were a jerk for insulting someone with a disability.

I came back to the chiropractor's office before work, before sunrise, and before the temperature rose above freezing. I nearly slipped on the long concrete staircase up to his door, but knew I was in the right place if I fell and threw my back out. I entered the office, took off my gloves, and signed a crooked signature on the sheet at the front desk using my frozen fingers. Then I sat in a chair in the hallway outside the treatment room.

THUMP!

The sound frightened me, but it seemed to be routine around here. I'd heard similar thumps on my hairdresser's mirrors at three o'clock in the afternoon when the pizza place next door started tossing dough against the walls. A moment later, a middle-aged woman with a noticeable hunch walked out of the office. Dr. Jonas followed and looked at me. "Ready?"

I got up and followed him inside the room. I sat down on the maroon chiropractor's table, which resembled a medical examination table but was divided into several movable sections that allowed Dr. Jonas to manipulate the bones of his patients.

Dr. Jonas sat down next to me holding several sheets of paper with illustrations on them. "First, I want to show you some stretches to help strengthen your neck and improve your flexibility." He stood up and demonstrated the techniques. I observed studiously and nodded my head in acknowledgment at all the right times.

"You can do some of these in the car. I tell my kids to do them while watching television." I silently thanked my father for not becoming a chiropractor. "All right, now I need you to sit on the table and hug your body so your elbows line up." I did so. Dr. Jonas put one hand behind my back and we leaned back together. Then he pushed me forcibly against the table and I could hear a popping sound emanate from where his hand was on my back.

"Good," he said. "Now lie back and relax." I did so as Dr. Jonas walked around to stand behind my head. He cradled my skull in his hands and lolled it slightly back and forth and then—CRACK! He twisted my neck sharply to the left, then again—CRACK!—to the right. It hadn't hurt, but I was grateful that my head still seemed to be attached to my spinal column.

"Sit up." I leaned forward as he pulled a fresh strip of sterile white paper across the headrest. "Now lie on your belly and put your face in the headrest." I awkwardly rolled around on the table, feeling like I was a beached whale, until I was lying facedown. "Just relax," he said, though the more I tried to relax, the more I seemed to tense up instead. Suddenly, the headpiece jolted an inch upward, making a loud THUMP sound as it pushed my head backward swiftly. It was forceful, but it didn't hurt. Now I knew what the source of those loud THUMP sounds had been. Dr. Jonas realigned the table, and we repeated the process four more times in an attempt to fix my forward neck curve.

Next he did some other adjustments that required me to lie

on my side with one knee bent forward. He rolled my body so far off the table that I felt as though I was going to fall onto the floor. Then Dr. Jonas forcibly pushed me down to realign some offending portion of my spine. I was impressed by his strength. Chiropractic adjustments seemed like a great workout.

"All right, next time we'll just do the adjustments instead of going over the stretches, too, so the appointment will be shorter," he said. It had taken only a few minutes to jolt my bones around, surprisingly quick for a doctor's appointment. Unfortunately, I didn't notice any change in my headache. "Now if you'll step into this other room, we'll try some therapy." I grabbed my purse off the floor and walked across the hallway to a darkly lit room. I could see two examination tables and another strange device that looked like a relic from the Spanish Inquisition. There were bottles of unfamiliar mineral supplements on a shelf lining the back wall.

Dr. Jonas left and soon his partner, Dr. Tom, came into the room. He was the middle-aged man who'd taken my x-rays at the previous appointment. As we made the usual small talk about the weather and the state of the economy, he grabbed two square pads that were attached by wires to an electrical device that resembled an amplifier. He disinfected the pads with a spray bottle and then placed them on the back of my neck. He quickly slipped a pillow roll behind them and told me to lie back on the table. He put another pillow roll beneath my feet and then started adjusting the knobs on the device.

"All righty. No reason to be scared! This device is gonna send a small amount of electricity into those pads. Very, very small! No worries!" His reassurances only made me more nervous. "We want to get the intensity up to the highest point that's tolerable. So don't be shy! Just lemme know when to stop." He started turning up the knob. After the fourth click I felt a familiar vibration on my neck, as I had during the first acupuncture treatment. He went up another three clicks until I said, "That's good." Then Dr. Tom left the room and left me with my thoughts and an unknown amount of voltage running through my head.

I drifted into a state of half sleep, which was welcome because sleep was on the top of my list of things I'd rather be doing at seven-thirty in the morning. After ten minutes, the device made a long beeping sound and the vibration stopped, alerting Dr. Tom to return and unplug me. The treatment had been slightly pleasant, but I still didn't notice any change in my headache. At least it hadn't gotten worse. I paid the receptionist at the door.

As I ran the magnetic strip of my credit card through the machine, I felt as though I were throwing $38.17 into a wishing well as I whispered my desire for a cure. It would likely be as effective. Though I'd been dazzled by his math at first, the chiropractor now seemed like an alchemist, mixing just enough mathematical and scientific jargon into his explanations to sound convincing to his patients and to himself. I felt bad for thinking this because one of my blog readers was a chiropractor and she'd always left nice comments on my site. I knew many people swore by their chiropractors, but I doubted I was going to become one of them. Perhaps I would have felt differently if he were treating me for a back problem or a slipped disk, but it seemed less likely that chiropractic treatment could cure my mystery headache.

None of it appeared to matter, because there was nowhere in town left to go. I would drag myself to these appointments in the cold, dark early morning, I would pay hundreds of dollars for dozens of appointments that I doubted were necessary, and I would do the stretches he showed me just to be certain I'd exhausted all possible resources.

For the rest of the day, my neck hurt even more than it had before. "Sometimes it can be more painful for the first week or two," Dr. Jonas said when I asked him about it. I wasn't sure if that was true or if doctors automatically made up rationalizations for why their treatments weren't working. When something wasn't giving me results, my practitioners usually told me to do even more of the treatment that wasn't working, instead of changing their approaches. When my first IV treatment had failed, I was prescribed another one. When I'd tried acupuncture, the practitioner said it could take eight to ten treatments. Did it really require all that time? Or were they just happy to take my money as many times as they could?

Oddly, no matter who I went to, every person was convinced that the answer to my problem lay within their specialization. The neurologist thought I had a neurological problem. The acupuncturist thought I had an energy flow problem. The chiropractor thought I had a skeletal problem. For once, I'd like to visit a doctor who told me, "I don't know what's wrong with you. Sorry, but it's out of my realm of expertise." I doubted that doctors liked to admit that they didn't know something. If I juggled people's lives in my hands every day, I wouldn't want to think I was capable of letting one of them fall and break on the floor. It was probably easier to cope with that job if you thought yourself nearly infallible.

I might have expected too much from my doctors. Yes, I wanted them to magically heal me, but perhaps that was like wishing Santa would deliver me a cure. It seemed more realistic to work with them as an equal partner to figure out what I could do to get better. We could share the burden and the blame.

The electrical therapy I experienced at the chiropractor's office could sometimes be relaxing because it resembled a massage, but it didn't seem to be doing anything for the headache. It was hard to say no to Dr. Jonas, though. He had a paternal nature that reminded me of a stern father who was looking out for my best interests. Some days I told him I had to get to work, and saved myself the extra money on therapy. Other days, I felt like lying down and trying it once more, especially when Dr. Tom laid a warm blanket on me.

"Are the headaches getting any better?" Dr. Jonas asked after a month.

"Um, it's not quite as bad," I told him, which was true, but that could have been due to so many other factors. I'd just avoided a round of layoffs at my job, so I was less stressed than I had been last month. The antidepressant my doctor prescribed recently might have been affecting my perception of the pain. I'd been better about exercising, which could have helped my overall health. Despite all that, I knew I'd said I felt better just to please him, because I knew he genuinely wanted me to get better. I wanted that, too.

"Are you doing your stretches?" he asked before cracking my

neck. Every time I heard my joints crackle and pop like cereal, I wondered if he was actually helping or just doing more harm.

"Yeah, most days," I lied. I'd done the stretches for two days and then abandoned them because I felt silly pressing my skull against my car's headrest in traffic.

After two months, I had a reassessment. Dr. Jonas measured the angles of my head rotation, all of which had improved, though I wondered how much he rounded one way or the other depending on whether I was the "before" or "after" subject. He performed all the same physical tests he had done during my first examination, pushing and pulling my arms as though he were adjusting a Barbie doll.

"Much better!" he said as I resisted his force. "See how much stronger you are because of the better alignment?" I nodded but was silently judgmental about the subjective manner of his testing. Wasn't he just applying less force this time than he had during the first appointment? How could he be sure I was really stronger and that he wasn't merely adjusting his strength to demonstrate the results he wanted? It would have been better if he'd made me pull and push against a weight machine, like that jungle gym contraption they had at the YMCA. It would have been an objective measurement untainted by a human who knew which outcome was preferred.

"How are the headaches?" he asked as he wrote notes on the small folded card on which he kept my records. I hated when he referred to it in the plural. It showed he didn't really understand what was going on. I didn't have headaches, I had one headache, singular.

"Well, not so great. I had a pretty bad one over the weekend. It's not too horrible right now though."

Dr. Jonas stopped writing. "Hmmm," he said, clearly disappointed that the adjustments had not yet cured me. "What else could be contributing to this?" he asked the wall. The wall didn't answer. "You work with computers a lot, right?"

"Yeah," I said. "I'm a web designer, so I sit in front of one about eight hours a day. I try to take breaks, though, and I've rearranged everything so it's totally ergonomic and reduces eyestrain."

"The electromagnetic field from the computer might be affecting your body," he said. "Do you have a cell phone?" I pulled my phone out of my purse. "Put it in your pocket." I did. "Now hold out your left hand toward me." I did. Dr. Jonas pushed down and my arm moved toward the floor easily though I resisted.

"All right, now put the phone back in your purse." I did. Again, we repeated the mutated form of arm wrestling, but this time my arm held firm against his pull. "See how that affects your strength?" *See how you didn't push as hard?* I thought.

"Oh, weird," I said. I was too polite to say *I think your testing methods are fundamentally flawed* to his face. I wasn't sure if my restraint was a personal trait to be revered or quashed.

Next he repeated the tests, but instead of using a cell phone he pushed on the area of my face between my eyes and right above my nose. "That's the vagus nerve," he said. When he pushed on my nerve, my arm was "weak," and when he released it my arm was "strong." Again, his method of testing seemed subjective and didn't convince me of the point he was trying to prove.

"Huh, strange," I said again. *Please let me out of here,* I thought.

"It can help if you carry a magnet in your pocket," he said as he opened a drawer in a small desk in the corner and sorted through the junk inside. He couldn't find one, so he told the receptionist to put in an order for more.

"We can get one of those for you, and I'll sell it to you at cost," he said. "Did you say you drink sodas?" he asked.

"I used to drink five or six cans a day, but I'm off of them now," I said.

He cringed. "Some of the toxins from the sodas might still be stored in your system. That could be part of it. Do you use artificial sweeteners?"

"Uh, I use some in my coffee, but not that much."

"It would be good to get off of those completely. You can use natural sweeteners instead, like sugar or honey or the new one that uses the stevia plant. You should also drink more water."

I really didn't want to give up my artificial sweeteners. I wasn't going to claim they were a health food, but they seemed to be blamed for all the evil in the world, from Middle Eastern warfare to viruses that crashed your computer. I didn't doubt that some people had problems with them, but when I'd gone off them briefly many months ago, I hadn't noticed any change. I'd also tried drinking more water, as Dr. Jonas suggested, but it seemed unlikely that I'd had a headache for ten months because I was dehydrated.

"Ugh," I heard a grunt from across the hallway. Dr. Tom was doing something to a man who was strapped in upside down to the Spanish Inquisition device in the therapy room. That made it final.

I'd earned my "piss-off policy" for the chiropractor. It was signed with that final "ugh."

I checked out at the reception desk and made two appointments for the next week. That weekend I called after hours when I knew no one would be there to pick up the phone. "I've been looking at my budget for the year, and I have to cut back on some things," I told the voice mail gently, trying not to hurt its electronic feelings. "Since I haven't seen too much improvement, I've decided I'll have to stop coming. I'll still do my stretches," I lied. "But I appreciate everything you guys have done for me. Thanks." That was the truth at least. I wasn't sold on their methods, but I did believe Dr. Jonas wanted to make me better. I hadn't gotten much for my money, though, besides the time to catch up on the latest issues of *People* and *Entertainment Weekly* in the waiting room.

A few weeks later, I answered an unknown local call on my cell phone. "Hello?" I asked.

"Is this Jennette?" the male voice asked. I confirmed my identity. "It's Dr. Jonas," the voice said as my adrenaline levels started to rise.

"Oh, hi," I said as I gripped the phone, pissed that caller ID had allowed this to happen.

Dr. Jonas asked how I was doing and how my other doctor's appointments had gone. I told him what medications I was taking. "We still haven't gotten to the root cause of the problem," he said. Dr. Jonas was not a big believer in medication. He again suggested I carry a magnet and let me know I could stop by anytime. I thanked him and we hung up.

The conversation had gone better than I expected. I doubted I would be buying magnets for anything but my refrigerator, but I appreciated that Dr. Jonas had followed up with me instead of letting my case dangle like a loose thread. Very few of my doctors had bothered with that courtesy or demonstrated that kind of care. I remembered the chaos at the allergist's office and the long waits at my general practitioner's office, which made me suspect many of my doctors were overworked and overburdened and had little time to follow up, even if they wanted to.

I still wasn't sure what to think of chiropractors, but I decided I liked Dr. Jonas, if not his treatments. At least he seemed to care.

I tried to get lost in the routine of my life. I hadn't signed up for any races or gotten involved in any community activities, as I would have done if I weren't in pain, so my life had become rather repetitive. This allowed me to notice variations in my mood that I couldn't blame on the stress of any one particular activity. Excerpts from my headache diary at this time, if I'd had the energy to keep one, would have looked like this:

Monday

Wake up. Drive to work. Feel like crap. Try to work. Drive home. Sit on couch. Moan. Go to bed. Moan. Fall asleep.

Tuesday

Wake up. Drive to work. Feel like crap. Try to work. Drive home. Lie on floor. Moan. Go to bed. Moan. Fall asleep.

Wednesday

Wake up. Drive to work. Feel like old sneaker with dog crap on the bottom, but not like crap itself. Maybe this roller coaster of despair is coming to an end! Drive home. Run on trail. Go to bed.

Thursday

Wake up. Drive to work. Feel like crap. Roller coaster of despair is starting another loop around the tracks. Try to work. Drive home. Sit on couch. Moan. Go to bed. Moan. Fall asleep.

Repeat ad infinitum.

Sometimes I managed to keep a headache diary for more than a week, trying to find a pattern in what I was eating, the weather, or my activities that would explain why this was happening to me. The data was all random dots on a chart, as meaningless as static on the television. Some days I felt good and didn't know why. Some days I felt like crap and didn't know why. All I could do was ride the hills up and down and up and down again, wishing I could get off the roller coaster or that the ride operator would slam on the brakes. I tried to appreciate the good days and tune out the bad days.

I managed to keep up with my blog, writing at least three or four times a week, trying to keep my entries light and humorous. I avoided any talk of the headache, as if I could make it disappear by never speaking of it, just as ancient gods and goddesses were slain when humanity stopped worshipping them and forgot their names.

I came home one night after a bad day, sat in bed, and checked my email, deciding to completely forgo that night's round of moaning on the couch and just head straight to sleep. Luckily, the headache hadn't hurt the quality of my sleep. If anything, it had made sleep look far more desirable since it was the only time I was able to effectively turn the headache off, even if that meant turning off my consciousness as well.

Someone had left a comment on my blog, and I noticed that they had left their name and web site link in the body of the comment. I clenched my teeth. I clenched my fists. There were fields in the comment form specifically labeled for a reader's name and for a link. Seeing that information in the body of the comment irked me, and it was usually done by someone who had more interest in promoting a link to their own blog than in contributing to the conversation. Last week I'd added some text to the page asking people not to do that, yet it had continued. I decided I hadn't made that warning clear enough, so I had edited my site so the sentence appeared in bold. I thought no one could miss it then, but this person obviously had. I went into the site code and edited the blog so the bold warning appeared directly above the comment form. No one could possibly miss it now.

Ten minutes later my computer pinged to alert me of a new email message. I opened the message, which was a comment notification from someone named Meg. I knew her name was Meg because she'd put it in the body of her comment.

Every muscle in my body clenched up. I wanted to pick up my keyboard, hurl it at my monitor, through the Internet, and directly into Meg's upper lip. I wanted to knock out her teeth and bronze her incisors as a trophy for my nightstand. I couldn't see or touch Meg, but I could hurt her. I could beat her up with my words. I couldn't do anything about my headache, but I could do something about Meg and everyone out there like her, so I did.

Please do not put your name or web address in the body of your comments January 6, 2009 at 8:13 PM

Oh. My. God.

Please do not put your name or web address in the body of your comments.

I did not make this policy clear until a week ago. Those of you who did this before then, I forgive. You did not know any better.

I recently put this policy in **bold** in the comment disclaimer at the bottom of every page, right below the "Submit" button. Yet people still left their names and web addresses in the body of comments. I privately emailed them and asked them to stop doing this. They apologized and I forgave them.

Tonight I added another disclaimer, right above the body section of the comment, just in case people didn't scroll down all the way to see the other disclaimer. And yet, again, someone just left their name in the body of the comment.

So now, I am writing this post, and I am asking you, for the love of all that is holy or unholy in this universe, **DO NOT PUT YOUR NAME OR WEB ADDRESS IN THE BODY OF YOUR**

COMMENTS. There are fields for that data. Putting them in the body is redundant. It pisses me off. It makes me want to murder you and everyone you have ever loved, including that boy you kissed in elementary school.

And I know, as I write this, that many of you will be mumbling to yourselves, "Wow, Jennette has finally lost her shit, hasn't she?" Yes, yes, I have. If you haven't been able to read between the lines of this blog, my life has been a miserable ball of crap recently. I am hanging on by a thread. And when you blatantly disregard a reasonable request that I have made easy for you to read, I am about THIS close to finally snapping and running through the streets in my pajamas, screaming.

So, please do not be the person who finally pushes my school bus over the edge of a cliff. Leave that to the unfortunate asshole who cuts me off in traffic tomorrow. And before anyone asks, yes, I am seeking professional help and, yes, I am on medication. I am doing my best to get by right now, but you are NOT helping me when you sign your name and web address in the comments. I know this is a stupid, stupid, stupid thing to get angry about, and the rage it has induced in me is a sign of my own current mental instability, but please, PLEASE, **PLEASE,** do NOT sign your name or web address in the comments. And please, do not even sign your name or web address in the comments on this entry as a joke. I will ban you and that will be it.

Thank you and good night. I will tell my doctors you said hello.

I published the post immediately, then started to rock and shake as I cried hysterically. I fell on my side in bed, crying until my quilt was damp. All it had taken was a stupid blog comment to crack my facade, like the perfect tap splitting open a diamond. I tried to pretend everything was okay, that I would make it through this. When people told me, "I don't know how you manage," I stopped myself from telling them, "Not very well. I'll probably kill myself eventually." I woke up. I went to work. I moaned in private. But I knew eventually the roller coaster was going to go off the rails, and now it finally had.

As I lay broken and bawling in bed, my hyperventilating slowly turned to chuckling. I had just totally lost my shit on the Internet. Thousands of people would see that I was completely loony tunes. People had often commented on my rational, no-nonsense approach to weight loss and to life, and I had just had a completely hysterical, emotional outburst in front of every citizen of cyberspace.

It felt amazing.

I had avoided discussing my headache lately on the blog because so few people understood how to talk to me about it. I'd been posting entries about my cats and healthy recipes as if everything was fine. It took a lot of energy to prop up that facade, so it was a relief to finally let it crash down. It might be okay to admit that my life wasn't normal anymore, to my readers and to myself.

I stopped laughing and let out a huge sigh. I felt the emotions sweeping out of me like a wave riding out to sea. Then I picked up the phone. I needed to call my mom. If I didn't, she'd be calling *me* when she read my blog that evening.

"Hello?" my mother answered.

"Hi, Mom. I was calling to let you know I just published a crazy blog entry, but I'm doing much better now." We talked. I cried some more. Then we laughed and laughed and laughed. When I hung up, I checked the replies to the entry. I was pleased to see that no one had left their name or link in the body of their comment.

9

Clinical Matters

To: Jennette.Fulda@home

From: JD@MoreFiber

Subject: Headache

Forgive me but this wasn't listed in your blog today and, when my mom was alive I thought she was nuts with this suggestion, but now that I'm 48, I think she was right. She used to say that . . . ok I'll say it, irregularity was causing my headaches when I was your age. In retrospect, I've learned she had a point.

I have followed your blog for over a year. Lost 30 pounds on south beach since Sept. Thanks for the inspiration, by the way. Anyway, the higher cheese/egg/lean meat and lower cereal whole grain thing brought back the headaches. Mom's idea, things like, forgive me again, dulcolax, helped.

If you've already heard this, my apologies. We must never speak of this again.

J. D.

To: Jennette.Fulda@home
From: Mac@SpiceWorld
Subject: Headache

1–2 Tablespoons of turmeric up to three times a day. Mix with pinch of ginger and cayenne pepper for synergistic benefits. Mix with smooshed orange or however you like. Some folks can't tolerate this much so work up to it. Turmeric acts like ibuprophen. Probably also revs up metabolism. Also, lately, over the past year, I've been wearing a weighted vest (you can work up to 20 pounds. I've used 20 pounds from the beginning, lengthening the time period I wear it in a day. At first it made my knees hurt after a few minutes, but now I can wear it all day with

> no adverse effects. When I walk my dog (three times a day for about 1/2 an hour) I carry a 10 pound weight in each hand in addition to the 20 pound vest. No headaches at all and I don't even need the turmeric anymore. I've never felt better. Also make sure your Vitamin D3 is adequate.

I fumbled in the dark, searching for the source of the chirping sound. Eventually I flipped open my phone, too incoherent from pain to be pissed at the person interrupting my midday nap.

"Hello?"

"Hello, is this Jennette?" a female voice asked.

"Yeah," I replied. I hadn't felt like myself for a long time now, but technically I was still me.

"I'm calling to confirm your 3:20 appointment at Dr. Reiner's next Monday."

"Dr. Reiner?" I spoke the name with a question mark at the end. Who was Dr. Reiner? He wasn't my general practitioner. He wasn't my neurologist. He wasn't my other neurologist. He wasn't my allergist. He wasn't my acupuncturist. He wasn't my chiropractor. He wasn't my ophthalmologist. Who was Dr. Reiner and where was he going to stick a needle in me?

"Um, what does Dr. Reiner do, exactly?" I asked, knowing there was no way to phrase the question without sounding stupid.

There was a pause on the other end of the line. "He's the dentist."

"Oh! *Dr. Rheinberg,*" I exclaimed in realization. I hadn't heard the name correctly over the phone. Dr. Carson was my dentist, but he worked for Dr. Rheinberg's practice. So the answer to the question of where he'd be sticking a needle was: my gums.

"Okay, I gotcha."

"Will you be able to make the appointment?"

"Yeah, sure," I said, now that I knew where I was supposed to go and whom I would be seeing. Then I flipped the phone closed and stared at the ceiling.

It was official. I had more doctors than I could keep track of.

If I couldn't remember every doctor I'd given money to, there didn't seem to be much harm in adding more physicians to my payroll. What good was health insurance if I didn't max out the deductible and test the out-of-pocket limit?

My neurologist had mentioned a headache clinic in an adjoining state before my last appointment with him. I hadn't been aware such places existed, but upon further research I learned there were several clinics that specialized in head pain. I'd put off going to one directly because they were expensive and more than two hundred miles away. Now that I'd hit up all the cheaper, local practitioners, I was desperate enough to cross state lines and spend serious money in search of relief.

I'd read about people's experiences at these institutes on the headache forums online. I'd been surprised that people in that much pain had been able to set up and maintain online forums, but there they were. I was a lurker on the forums and never posted or interacted with others. I wasn't sure why I'd never struck up a conversation with my fellow pain sufferers. It was just easier to lurk, read up on the information I needed, and then log off without getting too involved in other people's misery. When I'd blogged about my weight loss, I didn't start commenting on other weight-loss blogs until I'd lost almost one hundred pounds. I wasn't sure how long I'd have to have my headache before I felt comfortable enough to raise my hand in front of the class and talk about it. Despite all the suffering I'd endured over the past year, I couldn't quite accept that I was a part of that community. I could still get better, right?

It was on these forums that I discovered there were foundations and advocacy groups for headache sufferers. They even petitioned Congress for more research grants to investigate migraine disease. Headaches sucked a huge amount of productivity from the American workforce, as I had been exemplifying by researching headache clinics at work. The National Headache Foundation estimated that $17 billion was lost each year due to headaches that led to absenteeism, lost productivity, and medical expenses.

After days of reading about people's experiences on the forums, I concluded that every clinic was either run by arrogant sadists who would make my current suffering feel like a visit to a spa or empathetic caretakers who would listen to my problems and miraculously heal me of all pain. I suspected the truth lay somewhere in between.

I had narrowed down my choice to three clinics in adjoining states. A friend of a friend was a doctor who worked at the hospital associated with the first clinic, but the second clinic was closest, and the third clinic was in the smallest city, which meant it would be much easier to find parking. I was anxious making this choice because I worried that one clinic would provide relief faster than another or that one clinic would have a nicer staff who would provide a better overall experience than another. I wanted to make the best choice. I didn't want to have to start over at another clinic several months later if I wasn't happy with my first pick.

I researched the clinics online so I could make a more informed decision. I found out that the expert in the type of headache I was suffering from practiced at a clinic I will refer to as The Clinic, located in The City. I picked up the phone and made an appointment. Decision made.

A month later, I was pretty sure I was driving through The City even though I couldn't see The City through all the snow and ice attacking my windshield. It seemed idiotic to be traveling north in the middle of winter, but this January appointment was the earliest one I could get. It was also only weeks after the medical insurance year reset, giving me the rest of 2009 to rack up bills that counted toward my deductible. My first appointment would take all day Friday, so I opted to drive several hours Thursday afternoon and spend the night in a hotel so I would make it to my seven o'clock appointment on time.

I eventually found the hotel that I'd booked over the Internet. I discovered why it cost only $55 a night when I had to throw my body weight against the door to force it into a crooked frame. I was also disturbed to find a crime map of the area in the complimentary weekly newspaper, which showed that there'd been a car robbery at this location in November. I mentally reviewed the contents of my car to make sure I hadn't left anything valuable on the front seat.

Then I took the chair and jammed it up against the doorknob for extra peace of mind.

I dumped two folders stuffed with medical records and receipts onto the stiff mattress. I spent the rest of the evening organizing all my records and tallying my expenses for the previous year to see if they were over the minimum 7.5 percent of gross adjusted income I'd need to qualify for a medical deduction on my taxes. They were.

The air was cold enough to raise goose bumps on my arms. Even with all the lights turned on, the room remained uncomfortably dim, making it feel like midnight even though prime-time television had just started. I turned off the TV and heard the intermittent noise of cars roaring down the highway, but the silence hanging over this strange room was louder than any engine. I felt the quiet ache of loneliness, as if I were the only person in the hotel or even the only person in this city. I hated the paperwork scattered across my bed, but at least it was familiar, unlike this scratchy, beige bedspread.

I didn't know what to expect the next morning. I didn't know what questions they'd ask me and in what ways they'd examine my body. I felt a tingle of fear, like a cold stream of ice water being poured down my back. I didn't want to be in this hotel room that smelled like piss and bleach. I didn't want to spend money on an expensive headache clinic. I didn't know if this was the right choice, but I couldn't see any other choices left.

I'd considered asking my mother to come with me, but I'd decided against it because all she could do was drive me here. I couldn't send her into the doctor's office to give blood samples or describe the frequency of my headaches. My mother couldn't kiss the pain away. I was the one engaged in battle with the headache, and no one could fight on that battlefield but me.

Yet, as I put away my paperwork, I regretted my decision. My mother couldn't fight the headache for me, but she could have held my hand and sat next to me. She could have been a familiar friend in a frightening, unfamiliar place.

I finished my paperwork and turned off the light, so exhausted from the drive that I fell asleep within two minutes. Tomorrow I was off to see the wizard.

The next morning I walked past the hotel's complimentary buffet and had to restrain an urge to grab a powdered doughnut. I wanted to make my own waffles and drink the orange juice, but I had been fasting since seven o'clock last night for the blood test I'd have first thing in the morning. The hotel's sliding glass doors let me out into the coldest day of winter. My nose hairs froze in the negative-degree weather before I got past the guests' loading zone.

The clinic was located on the fourth floor of a tall office building in a shiny corporate office park. There were plenty of parking spaces in front of the building. At least I'd chosen well on that criterion. I rode up the elevator and entered a dim lobby that had warning signs outlawing smoking and perfume. I signed in at the front desk and was handed what I was always handed: a clipboard, a pen, and pages of forms.

I had started predicting a medical professional's ability to help me by how thorough their forms were. The welcome packet I'd received in the mail a few weeks early had included eleven pages to fill out. There were the typical data-gathering forms, but the packet also included a checklist of dozens of possible symptoms. Reading through the list reminded me that the human body was fragile and ready to break in hundreds of different ways. There were also six pages of medications they wanted to know if I'd tried, which left me with quite a to-do list. The welcome packet had also included a DVD that had been produced at least ten years ago. I convinced myself that this was comforting because it meant they weren't overcharging people to pay for slick, new promotional materials. Either that, or residents of The City still wore big hair and shoulder pads.

The rest of the forms currently on my clipboard were some sort of psychological analysis. I glanced around the lobby and saw five other people reading magazines or filling out their own forms. I wondered if they were in less or more pain than I was. How far had they traveled? I'd traveled a hell of a way since last February.

A nurse named Anne called my name and I got up. I peered over her shoulder as she punched in the code to get through a locked door to the offices, wondering what event had caused them to install such security measures. Had a deranged migraineur gone on a rampage? She took me down a bare hallway to a small room, where she took some blood and gave me a cup to pee in. She let me do the latter in a private bathroom. When that was done, Anne took me to an exam room, and we went over the complete history of my headache, tests I'd taken, and treatments I'd pursued. I'd refreshed my memory while sorting receipts on the queen-size bed last night. My conversation with Anne took more than an hour, which seemed like an awfully long time to be talking about a headache. When we were done she said, "Wow, that was fast!" with absolutely no sarcasm in her voice.

"Is it weird to have a headache that never goes away? Do you ever see people like me?"

"All the time," Anne replied. "It's not that rare, unfortunately." Anne didn't think I was a freak. I liked her already.

Anne led me to a conference room, which was dimly lit like most areas of the building. I sat down at a table next to a woman who was there with her husband. Other new patients started to trickle in until the seven chairs at the table were full. I devoured two protein bars I'd stuck in my purse for breakfast. A bald, middle-aged man across from me snacked on trail mix. I thought about trying to make small talk with my fellow patients, but I didn't want to be the first one to speak.

A woman with an angular chin, wearing a white coat and red glasses, sat at the head of the table. I looked at her name tag but knew I'd forget her name within a day as I had done with all the other incidental medical professionals I'd met in the past year. She led us through a new patient seminar that went over many things I already knew, including different types of headaches and possible triggers to avoid, such as caffeine, liquor, and smoking—better summarized as "fun."

The packet we were given also included a long list of medications and sound-alike or look-alike medications that they were sometimes confused with. I took note not to confuse my Celexa with Celebrex or my Indocin with Inderal, especially since only one of those was a suppository.

I did learn a few new things, like the SAT word "prodrome," which meant "a warning sign of an oncoming headache." I was aware that an aura was a prodrome of a migraine. Aura was the visual experience of seeing streaks of light zigzag across your vision or black it out completely. I hadn't known that food cravings and excessive yawning could also be warning signs of a migraine.

I yawned.

The handouts also said that people with weak necks might be more prone to headaches because a loose neck could irritate blood vessels and nerves that triggered a migraine.

I rubbed my neck.

The nameless nurse also encouraged us to get aerobic exercise, keep regular sleep patterns, and eat meals on a regular schedule. At the end of the seminar, they handed us all strips of paper that listed our schedules for the rest of the day. I was scheduled to see my neurologist next, then after lunch I'd have more tests done and meet with a psychologist. I returned to the waiting room and grabbed a cup of coffee before being called back to another examination room to wait for the doctor. A long, horizontal window spanned the top of the far wall. I gazed at the icicles sparkling down outside like prison bars.

I waited.

I read a handout about how to fight insurance company claim denials.

I waited some more.

I browsed through a picture book on the history of headaches.

I got some more waiting in.

Anne popped her head in. "Sorry, he's running a bit behind." Anne popped her head out.

I waited.

I checked my watch to see that more than an hour had gone by.

The door burst open and my doctor walked in, a sixty-something man with jet-black hair. Anne followed behind him. "Hello, I am Dr. Singh. Sorry for the delay," he said with a smile and an Indian accent that immediately endeared him to me, despite my long wait.

"No problem," I told him. It's not like I had anywhere else to be in this town. Dr. Singh set my file down on the table to my left and sat down himself, flipping through my history. Anne sat in a chair in the corner with a pen and paper to take notes.

"So, what brings you here?" he asked. We went over my history again in detail, using the notes Anne had made earlier to guide us. Dr. Singh then took me through a neurological exam, almost exactly like the one I'd undergone when they discovered a venous angioma in my brain. I looked left. I looked right. I walked on tiptoe. I walked on my heels. I got an A+.

"Oh, by the way, I don't know if this matters, but I did lose about two hundred pounds a couple years ago." The doctor and nurse would have earned a gold medal in synchronized eyebrow rising.

"Oh my, congratulations," he said. "How did you do it?"

"Diet and exercise over two years. The weight loss, it couldn't have caused the headache, could it?" I asked.

"That is very unlikely," Dr. Singh replied. "We have never seen a case of that, and we have seen thousands of patients." Once we'd gone through my history, he leaned back in his chair and rubbed his chin.

"All right, you were twenty-one. You were pulled over by the cop. You took Inderal. Six years later you were designing your webs. The headache returns. What changed?" He was talking more to himself than me, looking at the wall in front of him. His ponderings reminded me of a detective in a murder mystery. By the end of the appointment I expected to learn that the butler had caused my headache.

"Odd that you were given Keppra and Depakote instead of the more common abortives," he murmured. I had no idea if that was odd or not. In a war of the doctors, how would a commoner like me know who was right? I made the best choices I could with the knowledge I had.

"I should mention, your condition does qualify you for a stay at our in-patient treatment if you wish to do so." Dr. Singh explained that they had a wing in a local hospital dedicated to the treatment of severe headache patients. If my insurance approved it, I could stay anywhere from several days to several weeks, allowing the doctors to try multiple treatments until they found something that worked—hopefully. I wasn't crazy about taking two weeks out of my life to check into a hybrid between my college dorm and a hospital ward. True, I wasn't doing very well in my real life, but I was somehow sleepwalking through the days. Dr. Singh said we could manage my care as out-patient for now, as long as I came back for an appointment every month.

"I've sort of stopped hoping for a cure at this point. If we could just bring the headache down a notch, so it's tolerable enough that I can go about my life, I would settle for that." If I set low expectations, perhaps this place wouldn't disappoint me.

He leaned forward again and started writing on the papers in my file. "All right, here is what I recommend." Dr. Singh then advised that I get another CT, though this one was different in a way I didn't completely understand. It had something to do with veins or contrast or sticking a different letter of the alphabet onto the name of the test. The clinic would schedule the appointment for me at my local hospital. He then adjusted my meds, adding new medications, getting rid of old ones, or changing the dosage. I would be trying a new beta-blocker called nadolol and adding a tricyclic antidepressant called nortriptyline. He also prescribed two abortive medications to take when the headache was bad: metaxalone, a muscle relaxant, and Midrin, a combination of several medicines. All this time, Anne scribbled furiously, taking notes.

When Dr. Singh was finished, I thanked him and shook his hand.

"Is your job ever depressing?" I asked. "You know, since so many people never get cured. Is it a downer if people don't get better?"

"It would be depressing if people did not get better. But most people do, even if they are not completely cured," he said. I smiled. A warm feeling was spreading inside of me that I barely recognized. I think it was hope.

When I checked my watch, I saw that he'd spent more than an hour with me. I'd never had a doctor's full attention for an hour before. No wonder this place was expensive. Anne wrote out all the instructions Dr. Singh had gone over in the appointment so I wouldn't forget what he'd said by the time I'd digested lunch. She also gave me handouts for each of the medications he prescribed, which listed the various names they went by, how to use the medication, and any possible side effects. These people were fastidiously thorough.

I was then free to scour the streets of The City for lunch. During my search for food, I admired the turn-of-the-century architecture of the surrounding buildings and stopped at a quaint coffee shop for a bagel sandwich. I suspected I would rather like this town if it weren't coated in a layer of ice. I sat alone at a table near the window, feeling the cold seeping in through the glass. I reflected on the day so far and decided this journey into the frozen tundra was going pretty well so far, assuming I didn't get frostbite on the walk back to my car.

I returned to the clinic an hour later, traveled up the elevator, and sat in the waiting room once again. There were new people there, as well as some of my compatriots from the new patient seminar. "I just don't like how he talked to me," a man in the corner mumbled to his wife. I glanced up, glad that I hadn't had any problems with my doctor.

Laurie was up next, a technician with a Southern accent who led me to a room with a chair similar to the kind you'd find at a dentist's office. There was a rolling computer desk next to it and a machine with dozens of electrodes dangling toward the floor. I sat down, and Laurie explained that I was going to have an electroencephalography, or EEG, a test that examined my brain activity. I appreciated it when doctors took the time to explain what they were doing to my body. Not all of them were that considerate.

"This won't hurt anything but your hairdo," she said. Laurie began coating the electrodes with blue goop and then attaching them to my scalp. Her accent reminded me of the years when I had lived in Kentucky. We gabbed comfortably about work, her husband, and Craigslist like two gals at a hair salon. This would be the most expensive hair treatment I'd ever received, and probably the worst.

Laurie positioned a small light over my chair and then sat down at the computer. "Okay, look ahead at the light." I did so and watched it flash, first at slow intervals and then at faster ones. "Good," Laurie praised me. "Now I need you to close your eyes and hyperventilate for the next two minutes. Take rapid, shallow breaths in and out." I did as she said. After ten seconds I wanted to stop. After forty seconds I wondered if the two minutes were up yet. My fingers started to feel tingly. After what must have been two minutes, she finally told me to stop. I sat in the chair with my eyes closed. I opened them briefly only to be told to keep them shut.

Finally, the test was over, and I was taken to another room for an electrocardiogram, or EKG, which would look at my heart activity. I stripped off my clothes, put on a gown, and lay down on an examination table. Laurie then came in and stuck more electrodes on me, this time on my chest, arms, and legs. She turned on a machine, and thirty seconds later the test was over. I put my clothes back on, and Laurie dropped me off at the behavioral psychologist's office. I felt like a student on her first day of high school meeting all her new teachers.

A short man wearing a sweater vest stepped into the office a few minutes later. "I'm Dr. Strauss," he said as he sat in a chair opposite me, no table or other furniture blocking the space between us. I guessed this was intentional to remove any obstacles between us and promote an open atmosphere. "How's the temperature?" he asked. "Are you comfortable?" I told him it was fine.

Then Dr. Strauss asked me lots of questions about my life and my past, many of them regarding the forms I had filled out that morning. No, I hadn't been abused. Yes, I had a good relationship with my mother. No, I didn't drink alcohol to excess. No, I didn't have a history of mental problems. I started to feel guilty for having had such a happy childhood. Then he asked about my father, and I was relieved to be able to express anger about his abandonment six years earlier.

"Do you ever worry?" he asked.

"Yeah," I replied. My mother was the kind of woman who always worried that she'd left the stove on. Some of that worry had traveled down the family tree.

"Can you talk about that? What do you worry about?" he asked.

"Oh, just normal stuff."

"Would you say you worry excessively?" His question made me worry about the worrying. I didn't want him to think I had obsessive-compulsive disorder.

"Well, if I'm on vacation, I keep making sure I have my ticket with me at the airport and that I've printed out directions so I don't get lost. Just stuff like that." He nodded. This seemed to assuage his curiosity on the matter, and we continued the interview. I had crossed my legs in ladylike style, and I noticed that he had crossed his legs, too, as if to mirror me. I guessed this was intentional because mirroring had been shown to make people feel more at ease in social situations.

Dr. Strauss would also let the silence hang for a few extra seconds after I'd finished speaking, which gave me an urge to say something else. I knew this technique could also be used when negotiating a deal, like a car sale, to make the buyer think his offer was too low. He would then talk himself up to a higher price. I was glad I wasn't selling Dr. Strauss my car.

The last time I'd been to a therapist was in fourth grade. I'd been sent to talk to the school counselor because my family was moving again. I went twice, getting a piece of candy each time, before she deemed me healthy and I returned to the playground. I had come into this appointment with an open mind, knowing that the doctor's aim was to help me. However, I felt uncomfortable, and it had nothing to do with the room temperature. It was odd to be sharing so much of myself when I knew next to nothing about the man across from me. I wanted to get the most out of this appointment, but I felt a growing urge to bolt for the door.

"Are you in a relationship?" he asked.

"No."

"When was the last time you were in a serious relationship?"

"Uh. . . ." My eyes looked up as if the answer were written on the ceiling tiles. The real answer was "never," but I didn't want to talk about that. The fact that I didn't want to talk about it probably meant I really should be talking about it, but I didn't care. "Let's see . . . it was two years ago?" I said questioningly, as if I were calculating the time since a breakup, when in fact I was trying to stop myself from telling the doctor, "You wouldn't know him. He goes to another school. In fact, he lives in Canada. He goes to another school in Canada." I was afraid that if I told the truth, Dr. Strauss would demand that I start dating as part of my treatment. I'd read that people who were in relationships had longer life spans and were healthier overall. I lived alone with two cats.

Thankfully, Dr. Strauss seemed satisfied with my answers to that line of questioning and moved on. "Now, what is this here on your questionnaire? When asked what you wanted to get out of your visit to the clinic, your number three reason was 'blog material.'"

"Oh, ha," I laughed. "I was just joking." I had only been partly joking, but I didn't tell him that. I really didn't want my therapist going online and dissecting my blog.

"It's good to have a sense of humor," he said. "A positive attitude helps combat suffering."

The doctor made some behavioral recommendations that would hopefully alleviate the severity of my headache, if not cure it. He went over the proper ergonomic position I should sit in when I was working so I didn't hunch my shoulders. He told me not to use the snooze button on my alarm anymore since I was getting a diminished quality of sleep during the time between reminder alarms. It was better just to get up when the alarm went off. He also went over the benefits of regular aerobic exercise.

"Yeah, I've been crap about exercising lately," I told him. "It's hard to get up the energy when my head hurts all the time. I've gained some weight that I'd like to lose."

My psychologist then started to give me weight-loss tips. I tried not to give him a look of confusion. Had I mentioned that I'd lost two hundred pounds? I couldn't remember. I think I had written it down on one of those forms, but I wasn't sure if he'd read that. I nodded at the appropriate moments, wondering how I could interrupt him without being rude. I was fairly certain I knew more about weight loss than Dr. Strauss and half the population of the world, but I decided to let it go since I didn't feel like talking about it anymore.

Dr. Strauss opened up a file cabinet behind him and pulled out two sheets of paper. Printed on each sheet was a grid with seven columns across and five rows. Each row of boxes in turn had four rows marked B, L, D, and BED, standing for breakfast, lunch, dinner, and bedtime. I was to record the level of intensity of my headache for the next month between appointments. People's ability to remember pain levels was not very good, so keeping a record would allow us to take an objective look at any patterns in my pain. The scale went from 1 to 5 and was broken down like this:

> 1—Low-level headache which enters awareness only at times when attention is devoted to it.
>
> 2—Headache pain level that can be ignored at times.
>
> 3—Painful headache, but can continue to function.
>
> 4—Very severe headache; concentration difficult, but can perform tasks of an undemanding nature.
>
> 5—Intense, incapacitating headache.

Finally, the appointment was over and Dr. Strauss walked me to the billing desk, where I scheduled another appointment for next month. Next time I would just be seeing the neurologist, the psychologist, and the physical therapist, who wasn't here today. Then I handed the clerk my credit card and tried not to think about how much this out-of-network visit was going to cost me. I quietly hoped that I had chosen the best clinic and that I'd get results here. No matter what decision I made regarding my health, I always questioned if I'd made the right one. I wondered what the psychologist would have said about that.

I stopped at the coffee station on the way out, grabbing a decaf by doctor's orders. Two women were talking in the chairs behind me.

"I'm doing the in-patient stay," the first woman said.

"It's that bad?" the second woman asked.

"I've had a migraine since July," she said. I felt bad for the woman behind me, but I suddenly felt like a slacker. It had taken me a year to get to a headache clinic. She was five months ahead of me. If they succeeded in helping me manage my headache, now I'd feel bad that I hadn't gotten here sooner. It would have been nice to visit when the streets weren't coated in ice.

"Good luck to you," the first woman said. "It's not right for people to feel this bad all the time."

I could drink to that.

I drove home and reread all the directions the nurse had written out for me. I stuffed the four prescriptions into my pocket and headed to my pharmacy to have them filled. The pharmacist flipped through the pieces of paper as if they were trading cards.

"I need to see your ID for this one," he said. *Aw yeah, this shit is going to be good,* I thought.

I took the pills home, excited to take new adventures in brain chemistry. I was still riding the fresh hit of optimism I got whenever I visited a new doctor. I tried the pill I'd been carded for first, Midrin. It was an abortive medication. I was to take two pills the first hour, two pills the second hour, and one pill in the final hour. I did so. It did nothing. I still felt the headache, same intensity as always, but I also felt a bit buzzed. So I suppose it did something, just not the something I wanted.

Downhearted, I thought, *Screw this. I'm going to get some chocolate.*

I stared at the candy display in the grocery store for a few minutes before I grabbed two Cadbury creme eggs and a chocolate-covered marshmallow heart. They kept putting the Easter candy out earlier each year, which usually annoyed me but tonight made me feel grateful. I started walking toward the ice cream aisle, but standing in my way was a blond man in a black leather jacket holding a grocery basket. *He kind of looks like my brother,* I thought. I looked closer. *Oh, crap. He* is *my brother!* I palmed the chocolate in my right hand and waved at him with my left.

"Ha! So funny to see you here," I said.

"Yeah, just finished my workout," he replied.

"I like your new hair color."

"I like your new haircut." His basket contained no-sugar-added fudge pops, lean ground beef, and other disgustingly healthy items. Jim had lost some weight as well and was doing better at sustaining the lifestyle change than I was.

"So, what are you getting here?" he asked. I wasn't sure if he knew the answer already, but I looked at the tile floor feeling embarrassed anyway.

"Uh, I was buying . . . chocolate," I said as I showed him the creamy, partially melted eggs in my hand, too exhausted to try to lie.

"Jenneeeeette," he overly enunciated my name in a tough-love tone.

"I know," I said. "I am totally busted."

"You can eat what you want to, but yeah, you are totally busted." I put back the creme eggs but held on to the marshmallow heart. We checked out together. I never got to the ice cream aisle.

"Are you . . . okay?" he asked me as we were walking to the parking lot.

"As okay as I ever am," I told him, slightly slurring my words, and bobbing my head back and forth. "I'm on some new medication."

"Ah, okay," he said. "That explains it."

"Explains what?"

"You seem like you've got two drinks in you." I hadn't known it was that obvious. "Let me drive you home. I can pick you up to get your car tomorrow," he said. We piled into his car, and he pulled out of the parking lot. I lifted my right arm and palmed the top of my skull with my hand, reaching two fingers down to pull upward on my eye sockets, which I had learned were pressure points. I looked like I was giving myself a Vulcan mind meld.

"Uh . . . Jennette. What are you doing?" My brother looked at me as though I'd just peed on his upholstery.

"What do you think I'm doing?" I told him. "I have a fucking headache. I always have a fucking headache. This makes me feel slightly better or at least makes me hurt in a different, good-pain kind of way."

"Sorry!" he replied. "It just looks really weird, okay?"

"I know it looks weird. I don't care. If I'm in a car accident someday and they find me with my thumb gouged into my eyeball, you can tell the coroner what I was doing."

"Okay, okay, okay!" he said. There was a moment of uncomfortable silence.

"Sorry to be a bitch about it," I told him. "Just because I don't whine about how much pain I'm in all the time doesn't mean I'm not in pain all the time, okay?"

"I know. I'm sorry. I wish I could do something." I wished he could do something, too. I wished the stupid medication had worked. I wished I could stop wishing.

"No one can do anything, Jim." I sighed. "It gets easier once you accept that."

"The pills, they do nothing," I instant-messaged Sarah at work. She had been doing much better since her trip to the ER. She had entered counseling, and things were looking up in her life.

"I'm sorry :(" she replied. There had been a lot of frowning faces in my IM conversations lately. Neither of the abortives the clinic had prescribed had succeeded in aborting my headache. The change in my preventative medications hadn't done anything to prevent my headache either. I had tossed the useless bottles of pills into the plastic bag that contained my collection of unused meds. I had hundreds of dollars worth of pills in my nightstand that I could neither return for a refund nor legally resell.

"So, are they just playing Russian roulette with your meds?" she asked.

"Sort of. They have me take different pills and see if any of them work." Phrasing it that way, it sounded very primitive. My doctors had specific reasons to try the pills they prescribed, but most of it was educated guesswork that would be proven right or wrong by trial and error.

"I take it they've given up on figuring out what's wrong, then," Sarah half asked, half stated.

I paused for a moment before I understood what she meant. I hadn't realized it until now, but I had long since given up on searching for an underlying disease causing this pain. There was no tumor, no aneurysm, and no dead twin living in my brain. I didn't know what the official name for my problem was, or if it had even been named yet by science. It would have been nice to give it a title, but ultimately naming the headache didn't solve anything. Naming the disease would only put it in a tidy little box, which implied we had contained it and could see its borders. The truth was, no one really knew what was going on in my head. They had yet to manufacture a box to contain this disease.

I was confident that there *was* a cause for this pain, but after my experiences over the past year I was fairly certain that understanding the pain was beyond the current scope of medical science. I might as well have been an impotent man living in the eighteenth century. There was no Viagra to fix my problem. Instead we blamed my headache on stress, food allergies, or the weather, just as impotence had been blamed on lack of desire, when in reality it was a vascular problem. I might get lucky and live to see a cure before the rest of my life had wasted away in pain, or I might die without ever knowing what was going on in my cells and neurons. The best I could do now was throw some pills at the problem and continue to pursue other treatments.

I could have been frustrated, angry, or depressed about this realization, but I had already worked my way through those emotions during the past year. Now all I felt was a reluctant acceptance about my fate. My horrible, terrible fate.

I explained my perspective as best I could to Sarah. She empathized and typed the appropriate emotions of sympathy, as any good friend would. I stared at her messages and wondered if people would ever stop feeling sorry for me. It wasn't the way I wanted the world to see me. I didn't want to be a victim of this pain; I wanted to emerge as a survivor.

10

Through the CT Machine

In addition to writing me prescriptions, Dr. Singh had recommended Botox treatment, just as Dr. Fairweather had. This time I decided to be proactive and fired off an email to my insurance company about their coverage myself. They replied promptly.

From: customerservice@Evil-Insurance-Inc

To: Jennette.Fulda@home

Subject: Benefits-Authorization and Referrals

--------- Original Message ---------

> Hello, I was writing to see if my health plan covers the
> following treatments:
>
> Botox Head Injection (for treatment of head pain)
> Procedure Code: 64612
> HCPCS Code: J0585 (botulinum toxin type A)
> Diagnosis Code: 728.85 (muscle spasm)
>
> Botox Neck Injections
> Procedure Code: 64613
> HCPCS Code: J0585 (botulinum toxin type A)
> Diagnosis Code: 728.85 (muscle spasm)
>
> If you need more information, please let me know.
>

--------- End Original Message ---------

Ms. Fulda,

We have received your e-mail request dated January 25, 2009. The procedure codes 64612 and 64613 are not covered under your medical plan with the diagnosis codes listed.

Thank you for contacting Evil Insurance Inc. We are pleased we could be of service. If you require any additional assistance, please call your Service Center at the number located on the back of your identification card.

Sincerely,

Ima Tool

Customer Service Advocate

Dr. Singh had also ordered another CT, so I ventured to the imaging center once more. I stood at the reception desk, staring at the aquarium, wondering how long fish lived. Were these the same little guys who'd been swimming happily among the old and the infirm patients a year ago, or were these their children? Could they be their grandchildren?

"Do you want a copy of the privacy policy?" the receptionist asked me.

"No," I told her. I already had a copy at home. I was a regular here. They'd probably let me open up a tab if I asked. This would be my fifth imaging procedure in less than two years. I was fairly certain I'd been scanned by all of their machines at least once. It was a shame that Superman wasn't real, or else I'd have asked him to take a look inside my brain and see what was wrong. Instead, I was left to be dissected by another machine and fill out the standard patient form, yet again. No, I didn't have tuberculosis. No, I didn't have diabetes. Surgeries? Just the gallbladder removal and the LASIK. Same as last time.

The technician walked into the lobby to get me. He was the same height as I was, but he had a gray mustache and beard. "How was the LASIK?" he asked as he flipped through my forms.

"Oh, it was great. I can see twenty/fifteen now." I looked at the clock on the wall as if to prove it, which would have been more impressive if I'd actually told him the time.

"I hear they can't do that with astigmatism," he said.

"No, not necessarily. I think it depends on how bad your astigmatism is and how thick your corneas are," I told him as if I were now an expert ophthalmologist. I was pretty sure I could fake being a nurse by now, so why not an eye doctor, too?

We headed back through the familiar hallways toward the room with the CT machine. "So, what are you in here for?" he asked as if we were in prison. I certainly *felt* trapped.

"I've had a headache for a year," I told him, wondering how many more times I was doomed to repeat this conversation.

He looked up from the forms. "A whole year?" he asked unbelievingly.

"Yeah, it never goes away."

"I had a headache that never went away . . . I was married to it for twenty years!" He laughed.

"Ha?" I replied. None of my other technicians had been this conversational and nonchalant. I suddenly missed the chill of their cold professionalism.

"Oy," he said. "I was saying up front, you could have come at five-thirty. Just been waiting."

"Oh, uh, if you'd called I could have come earlier," I said a bit confused. "But the scheduler told me she could only fit me in at eight-thirty tonight."

"Nah, it's okay," he said. "Looks like there's a seventy-second wait after the contrast injection. That's more something for me to worry about." I certainly hoped so. I didn't foresee myself injecting medical dye into my own body.

I hesitated for a moment. I didn't want this man to oversee my test. I wasn't 100 percent sure I needed this CT anyway. My neurologist wanted to eliminate the possibility that I had a clot in my brain that was causing my headache, but even he said it was highly unlikely there was one. If there was, it probably would have killed me by now or caused other symptoms. I appreciated his thoroughness, but I also wondered if his follow-through was prompted by a fear of being sued in case this was the rare instance when I did have a clot and it killed me.

I had read a lot about the health care system lately, both because of my headache and because it had been a campaign issue in the recent presidential election. I knew that one of the reasons health insurance costs were rising was because doctors sometimes ordered extra tests that weren't needed. They did so because they feared a malpractice suit if you were the rare patient who had a condition that other reliable examination techniques had missed. I didn't think I had a clot. My doctor didn't think I had a clot. But here I was, spending thousands of dollars of my health insurance company's money taking a test that would probably show I did not have a clot. And next year I would wonder why my premiums had gone up.

I was also worried about the extra exposure to radiation I would receive during the test. I'd already had a sinus CT a year ago, the chiropractor had x-rayed my spine several times, and the dentist had x-rayed my teeth once a year for more than a decade. A friend of mine was a radiologist, and I'd asked her whether I should be worried about the amount of radiation I'd been exposed to. She told me that in my case I had nothing to worry about. She didn't charge me $150 an hour for her advice either. Despite her reassurances, if I did get cancer sometime in my life, I would always wonder if it was caused by one too many looks inside my body.

Although my intuition told me to go back to the lobby, I pushed the notion aside and followed the tech through a hallway. I'd scheduled the test and driven all the way over here; I might as well do it and get it over with.

We entered the procedure room, and I glanced at the same CT machine that had scanned my sinuses more than a year ago. I should have brought it flowers for our anniversary, or blank x-ray films. I thought of all the people it had scanned since then, all of the diseases it had seen. I bet some of those people were dead by now. I lay down on the table, my head pointed toward the semi-circular scanning device I would be pushed into. The tech started preparing the IV stand that held the contrast material he would inject into my veins.

"So, what do you do?" he asked. They always asked this. They must teach them to ask this during training.

"I'm a web designer," I told him, tempted to make up an imaginary profession to keep things interesting, such as "I clean up the elephant feces at the zoo. It's a shit job, but somebody has to do it."

"Ah, that sounds cool. I used to be in the wireless industry." I would have found that reassuring if I were a cell phone. The tech started to hum a tune. "I got this song stuck in my head all day."

"What song?" I asked.

"Uh, it's by . . . oh, what's his name?" *Thank you, Mr. Tech. I find your forgetful nature very reassuring as I lie here waiting for you to stick me with something pointy.*

"Is there an arm that—"

"Either arm. They usually get me at the elbow or near the hand. I have small veins and they roll."

He got me in one stick. Maybe I wouldn't have to file a medical malpractice suit, after all. I congratulated him on his technique, which he described in detail to me, which would have been helpful if I'd thought I'd ever need to draw my own blood.

"First we do the scan without contrast, and then I'll come back in and push the contrast into you." My mouth felt strange, as if I had licked an aluminum can. I told the tech. "That's the saline I pushed through. When I push the contrast you'll feel warm all over, and you'll get the illusion of feeling like you've pissed yourself. Note, I said it's just an illusion."

"Oh, okay," I said, wondering if anyone actually ever had pissed themselves on this table.

The technician pulled up two wide Velcro straps that had been dangling on either side of the table. He closed them together, wrapping me in a medical burrito, so my hands wouldn't interfere with the machine. Then he left the room, and the gurney slid into the halo of the scanning device. Then it slid out, and the technician hustled back into the room.

"Important question, are you pregnant or is there any chance of pregnancy?"

"No," I told him. *My imaginary, unborn, mutant baby thanks you,* I thought.

He left the room, and the scan began. The gurney slid all the way back into the scanning ring, and I gazed up at a red light and a glass panel. I closed my eyes so I wouldn't get dizzy or jerk my head to look at something distracting me. The gurney moved an inch back out, paused, moved another inch and paused, and moved another inch as I tried not to think of statistics about the high rate of medical errors in hospitals.

The gurney stopped, and I waited for the technician to come out and push the contrast into my veins. I waited some more. Suddenly a light started to flash on top of the IV stand to my right that held the contrast material. I waited. Was the contrast going into my veins? The technician had said he'd come out to push it. I felt sort of warm, but was I just imagining it?

As if summoned by my will, he came back into the room. "You ready?" he asked.

"Yeah," I replied. Then I felt *really* warm, in my crotch and my neck. My arms tingled. My tongue turned to rust. I glided back into the machine for the final scan. I imagined myself a year from now, dying painfully of a horrible brain tumor caused by my CT tech. I would lie there, berating myself for not trusting my instincts and faking a stint of nausea to get out of the scan. If I lived through this, I promised never to have a medical procedure at night again. Better to risk my luck early in the morning when the staff members were still fresh.

Then it was over. The tech unwrapped me and took out my IV, wrapping medical tape twice around my arm over a pad of cotton.

"Now I just need you to sign a form." *Saying I won't sue you?* I wondered. Instead it was a form saying I'd received instructions to drink at least twenty ounces of water within the next twelve hours to make sure the contrast left my system. I also had to stick around the lobby for ten minutes to ensure I didn't have a reaction to the contrast.

"Does that ever happen?" I asked, unafraid to hear the worst now that my procedure was over.

"Yeah, sometimes. The worst I ever had, this girl broke out into hives and her throat started to close up. I had to run down the hallway to get Benadryl to give her right away." The tech escorted me into the lobby, where I sat for five minutes reading an *Entertainment Weekly*. A reality show about obese people losing weight was playing on the TV. I looked up from my magazine to watch a twenty-something female contestant cry.

"Ever since I gained weight, boys don't look at me anymore," she sniffled. "They don't ask me on dates. It's awful. My life is just awful." She covered her head with her hands and continued to cry. I stared at the TV and started to giggle. I tried to stop but couldn't, and was left hoping the receptionist wouldn't make a notation in my chart saying I was an evil person who liked to laugh at fat people. The truth was, I wasn't laughing at her, I was laughing at myself.

As a former fat girl, I knew she felt genuine pain and that I shouldn't laugh at her misery. I had cried in dressing rooms and similarly hated how life treated you when you had a big ass. Yet here I was, in a hospital waiting room instead of a dressing room, and suddenly my old problems seemed hilarious. If I could have jumped into the television set and traded places with that girl, I would have. I knew that there were people who suffered in other ways who'd probably do the same, like suicidal Becky from the emergency room last year. Perspective and attitude changed the way I saw things, just as my LASIK surgery had.

I watched the woman on TV continue to cry and feel sorry for herself. I felt for her, but she was accomplishing nothing. I wished they would cut to a shot of her at the gym, working through her problem and living the best life she could. That was all you could do. That was all anyone could do. My life was awful in many ways, but I had to make the best of it. I was trying to live the best awful life possible.

I finally gained control of my laughter and checked my watch. It had been ten minutes. Technically, it had been one year, two weeks, four days, thirteen hours, and ten minutes. I got up and walked out the door into the dark. Then I drove home, glad to be alive, and drank two liters of water.

"I wish I knew when this would be over, or *if* it will be over. Either one. I just want to know," I told my friend Amy during dinner at a local Mediterranean restaurant. She had been my previous "Best Friend from Work" at my old job. I didn't see her as much now, but we tried to have lunch at least once a month.

"Do you really want to know, though?" she asked. "Would you have wanted to know that the headache was going to last over a year?"

I thought about that. When the headache had first appeared, I wasn't sure how I was going to last a week waiting for my first sinus CT. Now I had somehow survived an entire year of never-ending pain. People were capable of so much more than they thought they were. I'd learned this when I'd lost two hundred pounds, and now I was learning it again.

"Well . . . I dunno," I told Amy. "When I was losing weight, I charted out my goals and knew it would take at least two years to get to my goal weight. That seemed like such a long time. It was totally depressing."

"God, I know. It's taken me two freakin' months just to lose ten pounds," Amy commiserated. Amy was an attractive, dark-haired woman, but like most women she thought she needed to lose ten pounds.

"I suppose if I had known I'd be in pain for at least a year, I would have been depressed, too, but when I was losing weight, I figured, what else was I going to do in those two years anyway? It's not like I had other plans. I may as well spend that time making my life better. But the pain has had the opposite effect. I *did* have other plans for the past year, and the pain has stopped me from living my life the way I wanted to."

"I'm sorry, Jennette," Amy said with the same emotion usually saved for condolences at funerals. I'd been sorry for myself, too, for a long time. It was starting to get old. "If it makes you feel better, people's lives get derailed for all sorts of reasons, not just disease. You know what they say. If you want to make God laugh, tell him your plans."

"Yeah, it definitely feels like God is laughing at me sometimes," I told her between bites. "Sometimes I get emails from my blog readers who are trying to guess my disease, like they're reading a whodunit and they're trying to predict the ending. I'm just not sure if there is an ending. It's like I'm running a race, but I don't know how long I have to go. When I was running the half-marathon last May, I felt like keeling over at mile ten, but I knew if I just made it three more miles the whole thing would be over." I paused to take a drink of water and then continued. "When it comes to my headache, I have no idea what mile marker I'm at, or even what the terrain up ahead is like. Is it all hills and level-five migraines? Or is it easy downhill running and level-one headaches I barely notice?"

"It must be like when you get stuck in a traffic jam and have no idea how long you'll be delayed, or what's causing the delay in the first place. It's completely nerve-racking. I hate that." Amy was a veteran commuter who had a one-hour trip to work each way.

"I just wish someone would tell me how this story is going to turn out. Is this it? Am I going to be sick for my whole life? Or will I get better eventually? I've read that some women's headaches go away when they have a baby or once they hit menopause because of hormonal changes. If someone could just tell me definitely, 'You're going to be in pain until you're fifty-two, but then you'll feel fine and you won't have to buy tampons anymore either,' I think I could deal with that. Not knowing is driving me crazy."

"I understand," Amy said while I dug into my couscous. "You know, when I was diagnosed with diabetes I was really scared, but at least I knew what diabetes is. I hate having to test my blood sugar all the time, but at least I know what I can expect for the rest of my life."

"Yeah, at least you have a disease with a name that people understand. Whenever I tell people I've had a headache for over a year they look at me like I told them I have a third nipple. They give me this 'Seriously?' look. I end up having to educate them about headaches and then telling them that 'Yes, I tried this and yes, I tried that. Blah, blah, blah, shut up, please.' I might just start telling people I have multiple sclerosis or fibromyalgia or something, so we can all shut up about the goddamn headache, already."

Amy cringed. "I'm sorry," she said. "We don't have to talk about it."

"No, it's okay," I replied. "I kind of like talking about it with you. You seem to understand what it's like, because of your diabetes. You don't try to fix me."

"That's because I don't think you're broken," Amy said.

I smiled. "I'm just broke, right?" We giggled. There had been a forced one-week furlough at my workplace that month. I had somehow managed to build a decent savings account despite the medical bills, but the unpaid time off had put a small dent in it.

"I don't know, Jennette," Amy said hesitantly. "I don't want to give you false hope, or be one of those people who annoy you by giving you advice, but I just think a year from now this is all going to be in the past."

"Technically that is true of everything," I said as I poked at the couscous on my plate.

Amy rolled her eyes. "You know what I mean. I think this period of your life is going to be like the years when you were morbidly obese. One day it's going to be over, and you'll look back on it remembering it like it happened to someone else. It will just be this funny story you tell people."

"Amy, that would be awesome, but I'm not going to get my

hopes up. That way they can't come crashing down." I took a big chomp of my Greek salad. It was delicious.

"And I don't want you to," Amy replied. "I'm not a psychic. I just have good vibes about this."

I played with my food a little but couldn't help smiling reluctantly. "Thanks," I told her. Usually when people made comments about my disease, they couldn't help but step on a land mine. Yet I wanted to believe Amy's prophecy, partially because she hadn't actually wished to cure me, only that I would be able to put all this behind me someday. I was beginning to realize I did not necessarily need to be cured to move on with my life. Ever since I'd gone to the pain seminar, I'd been ruminating on the concept of pain versus suffering. I hadn't pursued it that far because I'd kept myself distracted with doctor visits, but it felt as though there was an answer in there somewhere, even if I didn't know what the question was. Instead of living *in* pain, perhaps I could learn to live *with* pain, as if it were my partner instead of my master. It would always be there, but I didn't have to let it boss me around. I might always be in pain, but I didn't necessarily always have to suffer.

I took a bite of a juicy olive. I admired the photos of Italy and France hanging on the fresco walls of the restaurant. I hoped to visit those places someday. I looked at Amy as she devoured the spinach-and-mushroom omelet she adored. *This is a good moment,* I thought. I could admire the good moments when they came, roll them around in my mouth like a juicy olive, and hold on to the taste long after the meal was done.

"Have you been feeling any better at all since you went to that appointment at the headache clinic?" Amy asked.

"Well, maybe. I don't know."

"You don't know?" Amy asked, confused.

"Pain is so weird," I told her. "Technically, all pain is perceived in your brain, you know? Like those people with phantom limb syndrome? They no longer have an arm or a leg, but they can still feel pain in them. That's because the nerve pathways from their brains to their limbs are still there, although they're incomplete. They're just malfunctioning in some way."

"Sure," Amy said. "It's like how bugs can still twitch around for a while after you kill them."

"Uh, I don't think so," I replied. "I think that's something else."

"Oh, okay," Amy replied. "We shouldn't talk about bugs while we're eating anyway."

"No kidding," I told her. "So, I definitely still have the headache, and it's still awful, but I can't remember if it's more awful than it used to be. It's not like there's a headache barometer stamped on my head to tell me if my pain levels are rising or falling. Mostly I just compare my pain to how I felt yesterday, or to how I felt in the morning, and determine if it's better or worse from that jumping-off point."

"That makes sense," Amy said.

"Plus, I just expect to be in pain these days."

"Dude, that's so depressing."

"Yeah, I guess, but oddly enough it makes it a bit easier. For those first few months, I kept waking up hoping the headache would be gone in the morning because that's how my life had always been before. I lived without pain. I expected it. Now when I wake up, I expect to have a headache, so if my pain isn't too bad, I consider that to be a really good day. Whereas a year ago, if I'd woken up with the exact same level of pain, I would've been pissed because I expected not to be experiencing pain."

"You might be building up a tolerance to pain, too," Amy said. "I'm such a wimp when it comes to pain. Pricking my finger every day is one thing, but if I ever have a kid, I'm getting the epidural." Amy's diabetes complicated her chances of ever becoming pregnant, but she was still hoping to have children someday.

"Right, ten years ago I would have said the same thing. But now I'd just say, 'Bring it on!' I have no doubt I could handle the pain of childbirth. I mean, I'm sure it's awful, but unlike my headache, it would go away, and you'd have a kid when it's over, which I guess is good if you like changing diapers. Sometimes I'm actually jealous of people who have migraines because at least their headaches come and go."

"My aunt's had migraines that have sent her to the emergency room. Trust me, you shouldn't be jealous."

"Yeah, I know. I just miss that feeling of not hurting. The thing that sucks about pain is that it's so hard for your brain to tune it out. Like, if you walk into a room and smell something rank or moldy, after about ten or twenty minutes you don't really notice it anymore. Pain is *nothing* like that. Even though I've gotten better at ignoring it and filtering it to an extent, it's still broadcasting as strongly as it ever did. My brain never really gets used to it."

"Well, I hope you find relief," Amy said.

"Yeah, relief," I replied. "I'm still trying to figure out what that means."

That night I sat on my bed with five bottles of pills in front of me. I'd previously counted out my medication into a seven-day pill holder that had the letters S, M, T, W, T, F, and S printed on each compartment, representing the days of the week. Last week I'd walked into the drugstore and bought one of the mega, multicolored pill containers with seven columns and four rows of compartments. It was intended for people who had to take medication in the morning, afternoon, evening, and night, but I used it to count out all my pills for the month, saving me the time of opening and closing several bottles of pills every week. I had watched a story on the news recently about someone with cancer and had been momentarily gleeful when I noticed she had the same pillbox as me. Then I had been immediately depressed that this was something I was excited over. It had also made me remember that I needed to refill my pillbox.

My grandmother had owned a similar box before she died, which I remember seeing on her nightstand when I was a child. It contained pills for blood pressure and conditions related to her ovarian cancer. I wondered if my grandmother had been in a lot of pain during the end of her life. As I continued to count out the pills, I realized I had skipped becoming my mother and had gone straight to becoming my grandmother.

Like so many simple tasks, such as brushing my teeth or washing the dishes, taking my pills every night was annoying simply because

I had to do it every single night. I began my routine by popping a fish oil capsule in my mouth, washing it down with water, and then repeating the gesture with another fish oil capsule because they were too big to swallow together. The omega-3 fatty acids in the fish oil were supposed to be good for my health in a way I could not precisely remember. They were good for me, that's all that mattered. Then I had to take another swig of water to down the daily multivitamin that ensured I was getting enough vitamin D and magnesium, which were supposed to help people with headaches. Then I moved on to my prescription medications, swallowing my antidepressant and my beta-blocker together because they were both round tablets. The beta-blocker had a bitter taste, so I tried to float it on top of the water, never allowing it to touch my tongue, but sometimes I choked and sucked on the nasty medication anyway.

Finally, I took three capsules of a tricyclic antidepressant that slid down easily. I didn't take this medication for depression, but because that family of drugs sometimes helped people with chronic headaches. Why? They didn't precisely know, but they guessed that the neurotransmitters in the brain affected by the drug were in some way involved with my pain. I had often shied away from religion because its faith-based approach could be murky and uncertain, but now I was learning that our knowledge of science could be equally murky. The answers we sought in religion or science might exist, but they were trapped behind a foggy pane of glass that I could not clear. All I could do was swallow the pills and say a prayer.

I resented having to take all these pills every night. It was mundane and time-consuming. Yet I also felt silly for resenting it so much. It was an easy thing to do, and one minute spent swallowing pills was not much to ask of a person every day. Every time I felt the pills passing down my throat, I wished my body was not broken like this, especially since all the tests said nothing was broken at all.

I took my pills and tossed the container into the drawer with the rest of my medications, including the three-month supply of Topamax I still hadn't disposed of. The pharmacist said I could bring it in for them to throw out, or I could mix the pills with used kitty litter and toss them in the dumpster. The thrifty part of my brain kept telling me that it was wrong to throw out $80 worth of medication, even if I had no use for it anymore. This drawer contained the detritus of my illness, divided into gel caps and tablets.

I climbed into bed and my small black cat, Java Bean, leaped onto the mattress beside me. He flung his furry body across my neck and meowed. I petted his soft fur, and he purred. He climbed off my neck and snuggled in the crook of my arm, rolling about with contentment. My head still hurt, as always, but a cuddly cat made life a little bit better.

I turned off the light and went to bed.

11

Feeling My Way

To: Jennette.Fulda@home
From: Georgia@SuperSonicMigraineNose
Subject: I feel your pain

I feel your pain to an extent, well, not your exact pain but my own version of your pain. I started getting completely debilitating "migraines" 19 years ago. They or it has never stopped, just varied in intensity. There are times when I will wake from a deep sleep in tears and screams with pain so intense that all I can do is have some one drive me to the

ER for a shot of heavy duty narcotics to knock me out until it subsides into a more bearable pain level.

Most of the time I just have a nagging level 2–3 pain on the right side of my head. That is what I live with daily. It is worse when the nausea, photophobia, extreme sensitivity to sound and smells comes into play. I drive my family and friends crazy complaining about "phantom foul odors" that no one else can smell.

The people I work with think I am either crazy, a drug addict or a faker.

I have tried chiropractic, botox, every pill known to man, homeopathic remedies, altering my diet, I have lost 120 lbs, cut out caffeine, added caffeine in moderation, cut out sugar, ARRGH!!

I feel you. I wish you luck and am there to bitch about it if you need me.

Now I must go search for that horrible smell, I am sure a cat must have used a litter box somewhere. Super sonic migraine nose always knows.

To: Jennette.Fulda@home

From: Terry@CauseAndEffect

Subject: Headache

Hi Jenette!

Concerning your headaches (for which you do not want advice ;)); there was a time when you didn't have them, so something must have brought them on. That probably means there are things you can do to stop the headaches. Since you've made sure it's (probably) not anything physically wrong, you should look for unconventional cures. Of course, looking for answers can be stressful too. You have to know that there's usually a solution (or more) to any problem. I just have to make one suggestion, since you mentioned the headaches; have you tried Craniosacral therapy? My homeopath speaks highly of it.

Terry :)

There was a picture of a naked man on the hotel nightstand. More precisely, there was a brochure featuring a picture of a naked man lying on a massage table facedown, with a towel censoring his X-rated bits. A woman was standing with one foot on the table and one foot on the man's back while she held on to two bamboo rails hanging parallel to the ceiling. It looked like she was performing a gymnastics routine on an upside-down version of the parallel bars.

I had to try this.

I was in a Colorado hotel for the weekend on a ski vacation. I could not afford a ski vacation, which is why I was glad I had won one in a contest. I'd felt fairly unlucky this past year, but it was nice to know good things could still happen to me, like free ski-lift passes. I had also hoped the high altitude might miraculously cure my headache. It hadn't. In fact, one of the symptoms of altitude sickness is headache, so I should have been grateful my headache hadn't gotten any worse. The altitude had succeeded in making me dehydrated, not a recommended state for a chronic pain sufferer.

To get to the hotel, my brother and I had driven through the mountain pass of doom, at night, in the snow. This had not done any favors for the constant tension in my skull. My brother's foot had almost gone numb riding the brake down the 7 percent inclines, and the windshield had been practically opaque because of a faulty windshield wiper. This was ultimately for the best because my brother hadn't been able to read the signs that said "Avalanche Area." Nor had he seen the semi being loaded onto a tow truck on the side of the road. During the long hour we'd spent inside the rental SUV, I'd had to consciously will my shoulder and neck muscles to relax. Pretending to squeeze an orange between my shoulder blades was not going to get us through the mountain pass of doom any more safely.

Thus, the massage therapist's brochure promising relaxing massages seemed all the more appealing when I stared at it from the queen-size bed, my face enveloped by a cushy pillow. I scheduled a massage the following evening with the masseuse, Pamela. In the meantime, my brother and I skied, ate, and rode the gondola up and down the mountain. The scenery was dazzling enough to momentarily distract me from the unrelenting pain in my head.

Saturday evening, I walked down to Pamela's studio, which was a small room tucked in the back of the hotel gym. I sat on a bench outside the door, listening to the whir of the box fan that was pointed at a small vent at the bottom of the door. A short woman with a pixie haircut, a tan, and a bright smile opened the door and stepped outside.

"Hello there! I'm sorry that I'm running a little late," she said. When she shook my hand, I noticed the toned muscles in her arms and caught a whiff of patchouli oil. "Now, tell me, what kind of massage are you interested in?" she asked.

"Well, what are my options?" I answered her question with a question. Pamela picked up a pamphlet from a table near the door and pointed out the different services she offered, including hot lava stone massage and deep-tissue massage. This must have made me look even more confused, because she changed her line of questioning.

"Massage can be adapted for different ends. Do you want me to work on your flexibility, or are you more interested in relaxation?"

"Definitely relaxation. I've had a headache problem recently." I told her about my pain and finished explaining my situation just as a middle-aged man in jeans and a flannel shirt opened the door and came out of the studio. He had a contented smile on his face.

"Thanks so much, Pamela!" he said. Then he turned to me. "Sorry, darling. I was a little late and twisted up her schedule."

"It's really no problem," I told him. These people obviously didn't realize I'd gotten very used to waiting during the past year. I was beginning to think that a doctor's customers were called "patients" because they were required to be very patient while waiting for their appointments.

Pamela ushered me into her candlelit massage room, which smelled of incense. There were tapestries hanging on the wall and a soft rug on the floor. It was a room I would have felt equally comfortable smoking pot in while listening to Grateful Dead records.

"Undress to your level of comfort and rest on the table. I'll knock before entering," she instructed me before leaving the room and closing the door softly behind her. I took off my shoes and socks first, picking out the lint from between my toes out of courtesy. I folded the rest of my clothes and put them on a chair, wishing I'd worn slightly fresher underwear. I hoisted myself up onto the table and lay facedown, waiting for Pamela to return.

I heard the door open and turned my head just in time to hear Pamela yelp and see her jump backward in shock. "Oh! I meant for you to get under the sheet," she told me as she stepped back and pulled the door closed so it was open just a crack.

"Oh, sorry, sorry," I apologized frantically, now concerned about my own crack. I hoped she didn't think I was a pervert looking for a different type of massage.

"It's okay," she said before closing the door. I got off the table and pulled back the sheet I had been lying on to see that there was another sheet below it and I was supposed to rest between them. I climbed back on the table and covered myself with the plain, yellow cotton sheet and hoped I hadn't frightened Pamela so badly that she wouldn't return.

A moment later, the door opened and Pamela entered the room without leaping out of her skin this time. She walked over to the stereo system and started playing a CD of calming harp music, and then rubbed some massage oil on her hands. She held a bottle of lavender oil under my nose for a moment and let me inhale it. *Aromatherapy*, I thought. *That's something I haven't tried yet.*

Pamela then reviewed the 1 to 10 number system we were going to use to indicate the intensity at which she would knead my muscles. A deep-tissue massage was supposed to hurt in a good way. Level 7 counted as a good hurt. Level 8, 9, or 10 was too hard. I was supposed to alert her if it reached that point. "Good communication is essential to get the best massage," she said.

I was used to using a similar system to rate my headaches, though my doctor used a 1 to 5 scale instead of a 1 to 10 scale. I had mixed feelings about assigning my pain a number. I wasn't sure if what I considered a 7 was the same level of pain another person would label 7. I suspected it wouldn't be long before doctors devised a test to objectively measure someone's level of pain, perhaps by using MRI machines to monitor brain activity. Until then, I had to pick a number and live with it.

Regardless of the flaws in the number system, I had started using it at work, too. My boss and co-workers would sometimes inquire about the intensity of my headache, so I had jokingly drawn a "Headache Barometer" on the whiteboard behind my desk. It resembled a speedometer ranging from 1 to 5. I would draw and erase a black arrow during the week, pointing it to my current level of pain. Once I got above a 3, I changed the arrow to red.

Despite the fact that the headache was always with me, I sometimes wondered how long it would take for me to notice if the pain went away. Yes, it followed me around day and night like a lost kitten intent on scratching my brain out. However, I had grown so accustomed to the constant, dull ache that I was accustomed to tuning it out occasionally, too.

When I had first moved into my apartment, every sound had made me stop and turn my head as I looked for its source. Eventually I had learned that the intermittent crunching was the automatic ice maker and the thumping at midnight was my downstairs neighbor's sound system. After I'd lived there a few months, I noticed that there was no subwoofer sending sonic waves of annoyance through the floor. I noticed the same absence the next night and the night after that. Eventually I'd deduced that my neighbor must have moved out. How long had he been gone? When had the silence started? I couldn't say for sure. Similarly, I suspected that if my pain went away completely, I might not notice immediately because I would first assume I'd just gotten very good at ignoring it.

Conversely, sometimes I wondered if I was now hallucinating the pain, as though I were a mother waiting for her teenage child to come home who kept thinking she heard a car door slam in the driveway. I had talked to my friend Amy over dinner about phantom limb syndrome, but could I have phantom headache syndrome? Perhaps the headache had long moved on, but my brain just thought it was still there.

"How are you doing?" Pamela asked. She'd started by lightly stroking my back with the palms of her oiled hands to make me accustomed to the feeling of her touch. Then she'd started kneading my shoulders with more pressure, easing into a more forceful massage.

"That feels good," I told her. "It's a level seven." I hadn't been sure how I would feel about letting a stranger touch parts of my body that I rarely showed to anyone else, but the relaxed atmosphere of the room made me relax, too. Still, the dark lighting and relaxing smell of incense didn't make it seem any less odd that I was paying someone to feel my body. I hoped Pamela wasn't repulsed by the loose skin I had left over from my weight loss. It wasn't as bad as many photos I'd seen online, but my skin drooped and sagged in places where most people's didn't. She had probably encountered things I could not imagine while practicing bodywork, but I figured it was her job to stay quiet even if she had to work on an unpleasant body.

I kept my eyes closed and focused on the sensations flowing through me. I envisioned small pulses of electricity flowing up and down my nervous system that were stimulating specific areas of my brain, letting it know what was happening to my skin and muscles. My brain controlled my perception of the world, constantly interpreting signals from my eyes, ears, nose, tongue, and skin to paint a picture of the universe for me. I wished we could figure out how to alter my perception so it no longer contained the dark hues of pain it shaded on the canvas.

When my time was up, Pamela stopped, whispered her thanks, and then left the room. Once I heard the door shut, I got off the table and put my clothes on. My hands smelled like lavender oil and my body felt like freshly kneaded dough. I returned to my room, lying in bed until the next day, when my body would rise.

The next time I had a massage, I was stretched over a table at a bar, being rubbed by a drunken burlesque girl. My friend Amy participated in a local troupe that raised money for breast cancer research while also raising eyebrows. I'd stopped by the bar where they were performing to support her. Cheryl Anne, one of the other burlesque girls I'd just met, was sitting with me on the barstools surrounding a high, circular table. She yelled a question over the music that I couldn't make out, so she leaned closer to repeat it. "Why don't you have a drink?" she asked.

"Oh, just diet soda for me. Alcohol will just make my headache worse." I didn't bother to explain the history of my headache to her. We were in a bar, not a teaching hospital. I didn't mention my headache to strangers unless I had to, just as I didn't tell everyone that I'd lost a lot of weight. I didn't feel the need to tell my life story to every person I met.

I wasn't 100 percent sure alcohol made the headache worse, but the doctors at the headache clinic had said it would, as did all the people on the Internet, so I supposed it was true. It seemed the proper thing to believe in regards to my headache, so I believed it, though part of me wondered if it was true at all, or if it had only become true because so many people had told me it was. It was only a few years ago that everyone knew that ulcers were caused by stress, when in reality they were caused by a certain bacterium. Regardless, I'd never liked drinking as much as everyone else seemed to and was secretly relieved to have an excuse ready to explain my straight-edge status that didn't involve lying about Alcoholics Anonymous.

"You have a headache?" Cheryl Anne asked, fluttering her long, fake, feathery eyelashes at me. She immediately put down her drink, and before I'd noticed she'd gotten off the stool, her right hand was gripping the back of my neck like a mother cat picking up a kitten.

"Oooooh, that feels good," I told her.

"What?"

"That feels really good," I yelled, turning my head to the right to look at her. Cheryl Anne's eyes were closed, and I could see purple glitter in her eye shadow. She had an expression of fierce, focused serenity on her face. Cheryl Anne pushed me gently, yet forcefully against the table and started working on my lower back. The band continued to play onstage, and the crooning of the lead singer matched the feeling of ecstasy flowing through my body.

"Do you do this professionally?" I asked her.

"Mmm-hmm. I'm a massage therapist by day, tramp by night," she replied.

"Where did you—aaaaaaaaah—study?" I asked between pleasant moans.

"The university here in town has a program," she told me.

Cheryl Anne released me after a few more minutes and told me my trapezius muscles were tight. "You work at a computer all day, right?"

"Yeah," I said, surprised because I hadn't told her what I did for a living. I wondered what else she could figure out about me by feeling my muscles.

I sat down in front of a computer the next day (to my trapezius muscles' chagrin), and looked up the massage program she'd mentioned. I wanted to know more about massage techniques and how I could use them to make myself feel better. The program at the local university took six hundred hours to complete, and the tuition was $7,000. I decided to head to the half-price bookstore instead.

I sifted through books about Indian head massage and deep-tissue massage and bought a few books because I liked the photos. On the same shelf there were two handbooks about medical billing. I opened them up and was overwhelmed by a complicated set of computer screens and confusing scenarios diagramming how to code and submit health insurance claims. No wonder the receptionist at my general practitioner's office usually seemed irritated. College calculus looked easier.

I brought the massage books home and tried some of the techniques on my own body, but it wasn't as satisfying as being treated by a professional like Pamela or Cheryl Anne. It was also hard to reach my hand around my back to massage my problematic shoulder muscles.

Then I was struck with realization. I owned a Hitachi Magic Wand electric massager, which I had bought solely to massage myself and for absolutely no purposes other than that. I found the device at the bottom of my sock drawer, where it was stored in its original box. The box featured images of men and women massaging themselves with the foot-long, white, plastic stick with a vibrating head. I plugged the massager into an electric socket and tested the two variable speeds on my back. Next I pressed it against my temples and heard the sound of the loud motor echoing against my skull. It wasn't bad, but I still preferred a sentient individual over my mechanical friend.

Cheryl Anne didn't live near me, so I looked up a certified professional massage therapist, making sure he or she wasn't one of the "masseuses" who advertised in the back of the alternative press paper. I wanted to find someone who specialized in therapeutic massage instead of just stopping by a local spa. I scheduled a massage later that week. I would have to pay out of pocket for the session because my insurance didn't cover massage.

The office was in a yellow, two-story house that had been converted into offices. The sign on the door noted that an accountant and a divorce lawyer rented space here, too. My masseuse was Laura, a stocky, middle-aged woman who was about six inches shorter than me but looked strong enough to push and pull my muscles as though they were taffy. Massage therapists, like chiropractors, seemed to get a good workout practicing their profession.

I hung up my coat, and Laura led me to the second door on the left in a short hallway. Looking at the closed door, I felt a small amount of trepidation, as I always did before seeing a new health specialist. I never knew what I'd find behind the closed door, as if I were playing *Let's Make a Deal* with my health. Would I regret this choice or be happy with it? Would there be a new sports car behind door number one or an old goat?

Laura's massage room was darkly lit, as Pamela's had been, but there were no rails hanging from the ceiling. Laura had several posters on the wall that displayed parts of the human muscular system, which made the room seem more like a medical professional's workplace than a hookah lounge. Pleasant music played in the background from a small boom box. I stood beside the massage table, which was covered in a Laura Ashley sheet speckled with a yellow tulip pattern. I told my massage therapist about my headache and other treatments I'd tried.

"Well, for your particular situation, I would recommend craniosacral massage," she told me.

"What is craniosacral massage exactly? One of my friends mentioned it," and when I said "friends" I meant "strangers on the Internet whom I'd never actually met."

"The craniosacral system includes the brain and the spinal column," Laura said as she motioned to those areas on her body with her right hand. "So, craniosacral massage is a technique that helps loosen blocked fluids and ease pain in that area." She walked over to the far wall and pointed to the diagrams of the neck and head there. "I just want ya to know that I don't use much pressure, so don't worry about that. It's actually a very gentle technique."

When I'd read about craniosacral massage on the Internet, I'd learned that some studies said it wasn't as helpful as most practitioners claimed. I agreed to try it at least once, though, because I didn't have anything to lose besides sixty bucks. Laura left the room while I undressed. I hopped onto the table and positioned myself under the sheet properly this time to prevent mooning my masseuse.

Laura came back and rubbed her hands with massage lotion. I was particularly ticklish under my neck and around my lower back, but just like Pamela, Laura was able to massage these areas without making me break into spasms of laughter that could have caused the massage table to collapse. She moved her hands slowly and gently at first, which seemed to be the trick to letting my body get used to her touch.

Laura gently rubbed my scalp, temples, and parts of my neck. She carefully turned my head one way to work on the left side and then the other way to work on the right. The craniosacral therapy was rather wimpy. I preferred the deep-tissue massage Pamela had given me that hurt in a good way. The craniosacral massage took only twenty minutes, so for the rest of the hour Laura worked on other areas of my body. The hour passed by quickly, and before I knew it we were down to our last five minutes. Laura walked from one side of the table to the other, keeping one hand on my body at all times so I knew where she was. That way I wouldn't jump in surprise at her touch. She stood beside me and massaged the tissue between my thumb and index finger deeply. I moaned, but in a good way.

"You like that? That's one of the trigger points for migraines," Laura said.

"Trigger points?" I asked.

"Well, see, when you feel pain in one area of your body, it's not always because of tension in that exact spot. You can have tightness or tenderness in one part of a muscle that radiates out to cause pain in another spot." The diagrams I'd noticed on her wall had trigger points illustrated on them in red ink, pointing to the areas where they could cause pain.

"The other trigger points for headache are on the forehead

between the eyes, and at the back of the neck where it meets the skull," Laura told me as she touched the respective spots on my head. "And of course, there's the one everybody knows, the temples."

The music stopped and the hour was up. Laura left the room, and once I'd dressed I went out to the lobby to pay her. She reminded me to drink water that evening to flush out any toxins she'd released into my system. I grabbed a mint from a bowl on the reception desk and walked out the door.

When I returned home, I pulled out my phone and started slowly texting a message to a friend. Slowly, because my phone was two years old and it didn't have a QWERTY keyboard like the newer models. "Sorry. Can't make it 2nite. Head hurts." Normally I hated using abbreviations like "2nite," but the slang increased my typing speed. I sent the message to a friend who'd invited me to go to a St. Patrick's Day party with her. The only problem? It was a lie.

I'd just had a massage, so I felt much better than I usually did. My head still hurt, but my body was buzzing from Laura's handiwork. I was fully capable of going out to drink green beer (or green Sprite, if they had it). I just didn't want to. It was easier to blame the headache than it was to explain that I wasn't in the mood. I quickly received a reply. "S'ok. Hope you feel better!" I deleted the text, feeling ashamed of myself.

I didn't lie about the headache that often, but whenever I did, I felt extremely guilty about it. If anyone found out that I was sometimes dishonest about my pain levels, it would cast doubt on every instance when I really was incapable of getting off the couch. I also felt bad for all the women throughout history who hadn't been taken seriously when they complained of head-splitting migraines because it was mainly a woman's disease. The primarily male doctors told them they were overreacting, or that the pain was all in their heads.

It was hard enough to get empathy and understanding for an invisible disease that people tended to ignore because they couldn't see it. I didn't need to undermine my credibility by using the headache to blow off any activity I didn't want to attend. Yet I figured that the headache had screwed up my life so completely that the least it could do was get me out of the occasional party.

Three weeks later I had another appointment at the headache clinic. This time I spent money on a hotel where I didn't feel the need to barricade the door. I got to eat the complimentary breakfast, too, since I wasn't having any blood tests. The decaf coffee at the hotel said it was "gourmet" on the label, but my taste buds begged to differ. I stopped at a coffee shop on the way to the clinic and stood in line behind a woman and her shaggy-haired three-year-old son.

The mother was holding the boy's hand, but he kept tugging away from her because he was intent on crawling underneath a table a few steps away. "Keith, stop it!" the woman said in an exhausted tone that suggested she really needed to get her coffee *now.* "You can't play on the floor. It's dirty." Keith kept yanking away from his mother anyway. Suddenly she lost her grip on the boy and he tumbled down, banging his head on the edge of a chair. "Keith!"

the mother exclaimed, now sounding more awake than a double espresso could have made her.

Keith's face turned a bright shade of red as his eyes, nose, and mouth scrunched into a pained expression. He was so blindsided by his injury that he sat there for two seconds with paralyzed lungs, emitting a silent scream. Finally, he caught a breath and let out a wail so loud that I was surprised it didn't break the glass surrounding the pastry counter. He screamed, again and again. His mother examined his head, which was starting to form a bump but was not bleeding. She picked him up and hugged him close, the morning coffee forgotten.

At that moment I was jealous of Keith. He was in intense pain, so he had screamed to let everyone know it. He didn't have to hold back his emotions or try to stop crying. He had the freedom to make a scene and express his pain in a primal, brutally honest way. I wished I had that luxury.

I got my coffee and arrived on time for my first appointment with the behavioral psychologist, though I wasn't sure what we'd be covering. I was much more eager for my appointment with the neurologist, where I would be asking him for different pills.

Dr. Strauss ushered me into the office and offered to turn off the fluorescent lights. I thanked him, and he turned on his desk lamp instead. I wasn't sure if fluorescent lights aggravated my headache, but everyone said they did, so I decided to go with it.

Then he began walking me through relaxation exercises, or as I referred to them, my Jedi training. Sadly, I wouldn't be learning to levitate rocks. Instead, Dr. Strauss told me I would be learning to breathe. Having breathed all my life, I told him a remedial class covering inhaling and exhaling was not necessary. Dr. Strauss responded by informing me that I was taking shallow breaths from my chest instead of breathing deeply from my diaphragm, as children do when they're young.

"When you breathe shallowly from the chest, the oxygen and carbon dioxide levels in your system become unbalanced, which leads to fatigue and stress. When you breathe deeply, your muscles are being supplied with energy from the oxygen, and your heart doesn't need to beat as quickly."

I looked at Dr. Strauss and said, "You know, this sounds sort of familiar for some reason." I was recalling vague memories of high school band class, particularly the day when the conductor had banged his wand repetitively on the music stand while shouting, "No, no, you're not breathing correctly!"

Dr. Strauss continued, "Proper breathing helps slow your heartbeat, lowers your blood pressure, and causes your muscles to relax. It also prevents the buildup of lactic acid in the muscles and lowers the level of stress hormones." I had thought breathing exercises were designed just to focus your attention on your body, but I was glad to know the technique had a biological effect as well.

For the first few minutes, we concentrated on getting me to breathe correctly, which was difficult because I had been more concerned about getting to sixth-period English on time than about listening to my band director. I couldn't remember if my chest was supposed to be puffed out or sucked in during inhalation, but finally I found the correct rhythm.

Next Dr. Strauss told me to squeeze all the muscles in my face as tightly as I could for a few seconds, and then as soon as he said the word "relax," I had to release all the tension as quickly as I could. For some reason, tensing all my muscles made it easier to completely relax them because I was going from one extreme to the other. We repeated this for several other muscle groups, from my shoulders to my arms to my legs and fingers and toes.

Soon our time was up, and Dr. Strauss told me to practice the breathing exercises once a day. He also nagged me to exercise more. I walked back to the lobby to wait for my next appointment. It was funny that I had traveled more than two hundred miles to a special clinic so they could tell me to breathe deeply, eat healthy foods, exercise, and maintain a regular sleep schedule. These were all very simple things, not ancient secrets protected by expert neurologists. Put together, they were commonsense advice on how to lead a healthier life, headache or not. Yet they were also the things that got pushed off my plate in favor of junk food and television, the coping mechanisms I'd instinctively adopted. I wanted to be able to take a magic pill and get better, but it appeared that if I took care of my body, I would have less of a need for pills.

My name was called again, this time by the physical therapist. She led me to a room that contained an examination table, floor mats, a stability ball, elastic bands, and some small dumbbells. After an examination similar to the one the chiropractor had given me, she determined that physical therapy was not necessary for my situation.

Instead, she grabbed a spray bottle with a blue cap. "This is ethyl chloride," she said. "It makes your skin cold, so it's similar to putting ice on your head, but it's faster and doesn't leave residual moisture." I closed my eyes, and she sprayed my forehead with it. My skin instantly felt chilled where the chemical had kissed it. It reminded me of the compressed air bottle I had at home for cleaning my computer, which released a similar smell and a cool spray. Of course, the label on the bottle at home expressly forbade me from spraying my skin with its contents, and I'd been carded at the office supply store when buying it, which probably meant you could get high off of it, too. "Does that feel any better?" she asked.

"Eh, maybe a little," I told her. The spray bottle reminded me of the ad for No-Pain Spray that had been running every day before the national news. The magical No-Pain Spray cured little old ladies of arthritis and made them want to bicycle on the beach at sunset. I did not go for a sunset ride on the beach after being sprayed by the ethyl chloride, but it seemed to help a little, so the physical therapist gave me a prescription for it. Then she sent me back to the lobby, where I waited for my neurologist, Dr. Singh, to call me back.

When he did, I was happy to learn that my recent CT scan showed that I did not have a brain clot. I told him I wasn't impressed with the Midrin and metaxalone he'd prescribed. After more careful thinking out loud, he upped my dosage of nadolol, a beta-blocker, and increased my nortriptyline, a tricyclic antidepressant. He also gave me prescriptions for industrial-strength naproxen, indomethacin, and another muscle relaxant, tizanidine, to try as new rescue meds. I would have to go to a compounding pharmacy, where they'd make the indomethacin from other medications because the drug wasn't popular enough for any companies to manufacture it and sell it on its own.

Despite all the disappointments I'd encountered in the past year, somehow Dr. Singh still managed to fill me with hope that maybe, just maybe, this time I would be fixed for sure. I wasn't sure if this was good or bad. In some ways it was easier to let go of hope and just deal with my life as it was. There was no use in wanting something you couldn't have.

I sped down the highway for several hours on my way back to Indianapolis. My headache levels were increasing at the same rate my fuel levels were dropping. Holding the wheel for long periods of time caused me to hunch my shoulders and tense all those muscles I wasn't supposed to be tensing. I recalled the relaxation technique Dr. Strauss had showed me and tensed my shoulders as tightly as I could, then quickly relaxed them. It helped a little, but my headache persisted. As the white dashes on the highway flew by, I noticed I was tensing muscles in my jaw and forehead. I willed them to relax but found myself scrunching up my face again minutes later. This relaxation thing was going to be harder than it sounded.

When I returned home, I checked my mailbox to discover a brown paper package waiting for me among the water and electric bills. I ripped it open at my desk and discovered it contained a hypnosis CD and a paper catalog sent by my friend Marie. She was a blogger in California whom I'd met a few times at conferences. A week ago she had sent me this email:

Hi Jennette!

I've been totally fascinated by this hypnosis CD website and catalog for a few years (okay, 8). I have a few of the cds—one on Healing Your Autoimmune System and one on Boosting Your Child's Self Esteem. I have them all in nature sounds, and we play them at night for background white noise.

AND YES, I am totally nuts, and a California hippie. I get it. I have NO IDEA whatsoever if it works or what, but I like the sound and I like knowing that I'm "doing something" in my sleep. Anyhow, they have one on headache relief, and if anything it might be a fun blog post for you.

I'd like to send you one, not because I think it will really be the relief you're looking for, but because I adore you. And I figure you'd have fun with the affirmations. :-)

classical music or nature sounds, your choice.

xoxoxo
marie

I'd chosen classical music and now the CD was here in my hands. I stuck my fingernail under the edge of the plastic wrapping to open it. I ejected the CD tray on my stereo system for the first time in months. Most of my music was in MP3 format now, which made me feel ancient because I could remember the days when I had bought music on cassette tape. I was so old now, and sick. No one had told me this was going to happen before I turned thirty.

Relaxing piano music played through my speakers, along with a low mumbling that sounded like a record being played backward. Was this a relaxation CD or a secret message from Satan? According to the catalog, the voice was reciting positive affirmations like "I relax. I relax my scalp. I relax my facial muscles. I relax my throat. I relax all over. I smile. I breathe deeply. I feel peaceful." The company that produced the CD mentioned in the liner notes that they'd patented the subliminal message technique used in the audio track, which I guessed was supposed to impress me. They used a technique called "dichotic listening," which Wikipedia defined as a technique where two different auditory messages were transmitted at the same time.

I lay down on my love seat, letting my feet dangle off the edge, while I flipped through the paper catalog that advertised other items from the online store the CD had come from. I paused on a page that advertised a buckwheat pillow that was supposed to cure headaches. Personally, I thought it was best to use buckwheat in pancakes, not pillows.

I'd received a DVD from Netflix in the mail, too. Once the CD ended, I popped the movie into my DVD player and watched *The Hulk*, starring Edward Norton. The film started with Norton's character, Bruce Banner, hiding in Brazil, already stricken with his penchant for turning into a huge, green monster if he became angry.

Bruce was studying meditation and wore a heart-rate monitor to track his stress levels. If his heart started beating too quickly, the monitor emitted warning beeps, and Bruce would immediately try to chill out. He breathed deeply and tried to relax his muscles.

I imagined my headache as an invisible monster living inside me, waiting to be wakened when my heart beat too quickly, or my oxygen and carbon dioxide levels became unbalanced. I took a deep breath and let it go, hoping the monster would go to sleep.

12

Meeting Mary Jane

To: Jennette.Fulda@home

From: Becky@DesperateMeasures

Subject: Oh NO! Another headache idea

There is a pain center in my state that is using 3 day induced semi-comas to "reboot" humans with pain. A friend recently had it done successfully. Now if I could just convince them I'm in pain. . . .

To: Jennette.Fulda@home
From: Leila@TheHookUp
Subject: When in The City . . .

Both my husband and his father have cluster headaches, nicknamed "suicide headaches" for a reason. What helped my father-in-law was going on oxygen at night and during the day when it got too bad. He no longer suffers from them in his 60s but I fear my husband, who will be 32 next week, is facing a life dealing with clusters. I never feel so helpless as when I see him sitting on the floor in the bathroom, crying, unable to even look at or talk to me because of the pain.

On a lighter note, I see you are in The City (I was there last night!) and weed would be a VERY easy hookup (for medical purposes, of course!). Email me if you're interested.

Eleanor had told me about her coping mechanism over lunch at the Chinese buffet. My favored method of coping involved sugar, high fructose corn syrup, and lots of whipped cream. Eleanor's favored method involved a pipe, some weed, and a secluded driveway. A month later, I invited myself over to cope with her. I brought the munchies. She brought the marijuana.

I'd met Eleanor at a friend's wedding only a few months ago, and we were already scheduling illegal activities with one another. The headache had become an excuse to do things I knew I shouldn't be doing. The binge eating was unfortunate, but I could blame it on the constant pain instead of a weakness of will or character. Even if I'd never gotten sick, I might have gained back some weight anyway, so it was nice to be able to blame it all on the headache. Now I was going to break the law, not because I wanted to experiment with drugs, but because I was a chronic pain patient in desperate search of relief. If this ended with a surprise appearance on *COPS*, I hoped I could deceive the police as easily as I deceived myself.

Eleanor's house was at the bottom of a small hill in an old suburban neighborhood that had lots of trees. "Heya!" Eleanor waved to me as I parked next to her garage. It was the early part of spring, and it had just become warm enough to go outside without a jacket. She was sitting in one of two lawn chairs set up next to a small table. A circular, stone ashtray was resting on the table with two glass pipes sitting on its edge. There was a small plastic baggie containing ground-up leaves next to the ashtray.

I'd searched the Internet to see if any of the medications I was on could react negatively with cannabis. I had found an independent pharmacy that filled my indomethacin prescription and considered asking the people there about possible drug interactions. They had a large green parrot in a cage behind the counter, which for some reason made me think they'd be less likely to report me to the cops for asking about pot. I'd chickened out, though, and decided to trust that Eleanor would take care of me if I started seizing on her driveway. I carried a card with my emergency contact numbers in my pocket, next to my insurance card, just in case something happened. I was a very responsible pot smoker.

Eleanor got up from her seat and asked, "How are you doing?"

"Oh, okay," I told her honestly. I was still in pain, as I was always in pain and suspected I'd always be in pain, but I hadn't had to cry secretly in the parking garage at work for months now. In my world, that meant things were going really well. "I have a confession, though. I've never smoked pot before."

Eleanor did a double take. "Oh, wow! You're a pot virgin? I didn't know you were a pot virgin. I'm honored!" she said.

"I've actually never smoked anything in my life. Not even a cigarette. When I take one of those purity tests online, I always score as pure as the driven snow." I sat down in a lawn chair and heard the aluminum frame scrape against the concrete. "Some of the kids on our annual senior-year camping trip in high school smoked weed and got the trip banned after that, but I wasn't one of them. And I think the people who owned my family's house before us grew pot in their basement because they had lots of fluorescent lights and a small irrigation system, but that sums up all of my experiences with marijuana."

"I'm totally corrupting you!" She laughed. "Well, then, let me show you how this works."

Eleanor stuffed some of the chopped leaves into the pipes. She handed me one, then picked up the other pipe and a lighter to demonstrate. "Okay, so I hold the end of the pipe with one hand," she said as she flicked the lighter three times. Finally the sparks ignited into a flame. She put the pipe in her mouth and held the flame up to the end. "Ven you suct it like uh strah," she mumbled around the pipe.

"I'm sorry, what?" I asked.

Eleanor took the pipe out of her mouth. "Then you suck it like a straw," she repeated. She put the pipe back in her mouth, and I watched the embers glow. "Then you inhale it, let it rest in your mouth and lungs for a moment, and then exhale." She let out a smoky breath like a dragon. "I hope that makes sense," Eleanor said. "I've never had to teach someone how to smoke pot before."

I picked up the pipe Eleanor had packed for me and held the lighted flame up to the end. Just as I was about to suck on the tube, a gust of wind blew out my light. I tried again, and the wind blew it out once more.

"Let's go into the garage," Eleanor said. She pulled an automatic garage door opener out of her pocket and hit the button. The door slid up, and I stepped into the garage next to her silver Honda Civic and tried to light my pipe once again, this time successfully. I sucked the smoke into my mouth and then let it out.

"There you go!" Eleanor exclaimed gleefully, like a soccer mom excited over her child's first goal. I sucked in a few more hits of smoke and puffed them out. The song "Puff, the Magic Dragon" started playing in my head.

We walked out of the garage and sat back down in the lime-green lawn chairs. "Are you feeling anything yet?" Eleanor asked. This question was the same one that the doctors at the headache clinic always asked me about whether the pills were working.

"I don't know . . . maybe?" I said. My answer was the same one that the doctors at the headache clinic always got from me. "God, this is embarrassing, but I don't know if I'm doing this right."

"I'm trying to remember what it was like when I first smoked pot, but I can't really remember," Eleanor said.

"Ha! I guess you've been smoking too much pot," I teased.

"Oh, shut up!" she laughed in reply. "Don't dis your weed supplier!" We sat on the driveway for several more minutes as I tried to properly inhale marijuana. A red sedan drove around the cul-de-sac at the top of the hill. Eleanor put down her pipe and grabbed the bag of marijuana. She leaned forward straining to see where the car had gone. I looked at her questioningly.

"Sorry," she said. "Do you think they saw us? I hope they didn't see us. I'm being paranoid, I know. Pot makes you paranoid, but whenever I see a car go by I'm afraid it's somebody who's going to narc on me. This place is so hidden that nobody should be driving back here unless they live here. And the lady two houses down doesn't like me, and I'm always worried she might call the cops on me." Eleanor took another puff of the pipe, and I wondered if that was a good idea.

"I don't think they saw us," I reassured her. I did not feel paranoid at all, which was probably proof that I was not getting high. If anything, my head was starting to hurt a little more.

"Is it helping your headache any?" she asked.

"No," I told her. "But it was worth a shot."

"Well, I hope you find relief," Eleanor said.

"Eh, you don't have to do that," I replied. "It's probably not going to happen. I just have to deal with that," I told her. I knew

Eleanor meant well, but I was tired of people telling me that they hoped my headache would go away. If I had lost a leg, they wouldn't tell me that they hoped my foot would grow back. I would gladly welcome that, but as I had come to learn, neither scenario was likely to occur anytime soon.

The only people who seemed to understand how to talk to someone with a chronic illness were other people who were sick. I didn't need advice, I didn't need them to say they were sorry, I just needed a hug. Pain was lonely. I wanted someone to stand next to me and share my view of the world. I wanted someone to look over the smelly, rotting landfill my life had become and reassure me by saying, "Yeah, this really sucks." Ironically though, pain could be isolating. Pain made you want to curl up in a ball in a dark room. This wasn't the best position from which to seek out sympathetic sufferers who might understand what you were going through.

"God, I'm sorry," Eleanor said empathetically. "You know, I had a headache the other day and it made me think of you."

"You're not the first person to tell me that," I said. "It's like I've launched a highly successful public relations campaign creating a brand association between headaches and myself. Too bad I can't make money off of that."

"You could become the spokeswoman for Excedrin!" she exclaimed.

"Ha!" I replied. "Only if they want people to think their pills don't work."

Just talking about the headache was making my head throb worse. I'd gone to a dinner party a few weeks ago, and the first thing the hostess had asked was how bad my headache was. It was thoughtful of her to acknowledge my discomfort, but I'd glossed over the topic and moved the conversation on to other things. Asking me about my headache undermined one of my primary coping techniques: distracting myself from the headache. My friends were trying to be nice, but they were unknowingly hindering my methods. Besides, I didn't want my life to be about the headache, even if my life was all about the headache. If I ignored it, maybe it would go away.

I doubted many people wanted to hear detailed accounts of my pain history anyway. It was about as fascinating as listening to other people recount their dreams. However, when I did talk about it, the headache made me feel special. Whenever I mentioned my condition to someone I'd just met, it felt like I was admitting I had a superpower. I couldn't see through walls or fly, but I had the ability to create crippling levels of pain for years at a time. People remembered me. I wasn't the girl who'd lost almost two hundred pounds anymore. I was the girl with the headache.

We sat in silence for a few more moments. A bird chirped in the distance, and another car drove around the cul-de-sac. Eleanor leaned forward again.

"Do you think they saw us?" she asked.

I drove home from Eleanor's, fairly certain I was safe to drive since I hadn't felt high. I'd taken a few more puffs later during my visit and thought I was starting to get the hang of it. It had taken a while to figure out that I hadn't been inhaling the smoke into my lungs, just rolling it around in my mouth. I decided I'd have to wait a few months before trying to smoke pot with Eleanor again or else I'd seem like a weed leech.

I wasn't too terribly disappointed. I hadn't been lying to Eleanor when I told her I'd been feeling all right. Granted, I was experiencing enough pain that if I'd felt this way two years ago I would have said I felt like shit. But on my personal scale, the headache had often been worse than it was now, so I was satisfied with the discomfort, which was tolerable if not desirable.

My mood might have been due to the new medication cocktail I was on. The doctors had told me it took several weeks and sometimes months for the full effects of preventative medications to kick in. The tricyclic antidepressant I was on had to build up in my system before it was acting at full force. This was annoying because I wanted a miraculous, instantaneous recovery. I wanted someone to lay hands on me and to cure me in that single moment. I wanted to remember what it felt like not to be in pain all the time.

I wasn't sure if my recent good mood was caused by the pills, though. I had learned at the pain seminar that suffering was determined by your level of pain versus your ability to cope with that pain. Was my headache really better? It might be that my coping abilities had improved so much over the past year that I simply perceived it as less painful. When I'd started lifting weights when I was losing weight, I discovered that the pails of kitty litter I hauled up the stairs had started to seem lighter, even though they still weighed twenty-five pounds. It was actually my muscles that had changed, not the kitty litter.

I'd also gotten better about setting boundaries on my activities and not trying to do too much. If I went out to a bar with my friends, I expected to take it easy the next day to account for the pain. I put in my eight hours at work, but I didn't bring it home with me and I'd stopped beating myself up over my self-perceived poor performance. I was beginning to feel that my dislike of work wasn't just because of my pain, but because I didn't like my job. Last year I had considered quitting and trying to get disability, but now I was contemplating quitting to work for myself instead.

As a freelancer, I could set my own hours and lie on the couch if I had a bad headache day. The biggest hurdle was health insurance. It was early 2009 and the Health Care Reform Act hadn't been passed yet, so no laws prevented private insurers from denying me coverage because of my headache. They didn't like to insure sick people. It was bad for business. I had applied for an individual policy to see if I could get covered but had received a letter of denial that said:

> *Your medical records document a history of head injury as a child, ongoing treatment for headaches, a venous angioma, and depression diagnosed less than one year ago with ongoing treatment.*
>
> *Unfortunately, our current medical underwriting guidelines prohibit us from offering enrollment to any applicant with the above noted medical history.*

Then, to add insult to my medically documented injury, the letter continued:

Your height and weight wuld [sic] require a 20% rate up in premium.

We regret we could not offer you enrollment at this time.

It took me a moment to figure out what they were talking about when they mentioned "a history of head injury as a child." Then I remembered that I had told the nurse who took my full history at the headache clinic that my younger brother had accidentally whacked me over the head with a flashlight as a child. I'd only mentioned it in an effort to be completely thorough, not because it had caused me any problems. Now this insurance company was punishing me for being honest. They'd also practically said, "You're so fat that we'd have to charge you extra." I consoled myself with the fact that the bastards couldn't spell the word "would" correctly, so I probably didn't want them to insure me anyway. A year later, they confirmed their incompetence when I received a letter saying hackers had broken into their system and stolen thousands of insurance applications, which meant I was at risk for identity theft and didn't even have a health insurance policy to make up for the trouble.

Without an individual policy, my other option was COBRA, the Consolidated Omnibus Budget Reconciliation Act of 1985. COBRA was an extension of my current health insurance provided by the company I worked for if I quit or was laid off. Right now, I paid for part of my insurance via deductions from my paycheck, while the company footed the other part of the bill. COBRA would cover me for eighteen months after I quit, but I would have to pay the full cost, which was more than $400 a month. It had been so silly of me to pursue a college education and a career when obviously I should have been hunting down a well-insured groom instead. I started to dream up scenarios in which I married a well-employed immigrant so he'd get his green card and I'd get an insurance card but dismissed them as better fodder for a screenplay than for the story of my life.

I was registered to attend a national blogging conference soon, so I hoped to meet some freelancers and get advice in sessions led by entrepreneurs. When I read the conference program, I saw a session that piqued my interest: *Bloggers with Illnesses—You Are Not Your Sickness, You Just Write About It Daily.* I circled the blurb with a black pen and later that day sat in a sea of a hundred chairs with dozens of other attendees. We were facing a platform at the front of the room where four panelists and a moderator sat. The room was warm and stuffy because of the body heat emanating from the crowd.

The panelists introduced themselves and revealed that they suffered from depression, diabetes, fibromyalgia, chronic pain, infertility, and asthma, but as with my own illness, I couldn't tell this by looking at them. The speakers talked about their experiences and took questions from the crowd. After about twenty minutes, the bleached blond panelist stepped off the platform to stretch her limbs and massage her temples. She anxiously shifted her weight back and forth. I could have deduced why she was stretching and fidgeting uncomfortably even if I hadn't already heard her introductory statement. She was in pain. She was always in pain. Just like me.

A man at the front of the audience currently had the microphone. He was telling us that his brain was too big for his skull. I sat stunned. That actually happened to people? I had used that description to let people know what my headache felt like. Sadly for him, an operation that was supposed to help his condition only led to further complications. A woman got the microphone next and mentioned that she'd lost her sex drive after starting Celexa, and I raised my eyebrows in surprise. I was on Celexa, too, but thankfully my libido remained untouched.

As if chronic disease weren't bad enough, one woman's house had been hit by a tornado, which had led to depression in addition to her preexisting chronic pain. The next lady to get the microphone told us she'd had to sell her business because she could no longer handle it while being sick. Another man had gotten a terminal diagnosis, which was later proven to be wrong. I'd been longing to get a diagnosis for my disease, but at least no one had told me my headache was going to kill me.

I felt bad hearing all these tales of woe, but it was refreshing to know that these people understood how hard life could become through no fault of your own. The last time I'd been in a room with so many sick people was at the pain seminar I'd attended several months ago. I'd felt a connection to the people there, and I felt the same connection with the bloggers in this room, even though I hadn't spoken to any of them.

Next, a curly-haired woman in the row behind me was handed the microphone. She stood up as I turned around to watch her speak. Before any words left her mouth, the tall woman who was moderating the session said, "Do it. I dare you to do it." I turned my attention to the front of the room, wondering what she was talking about.

"You want me to?" the curly-haired audience member replied.

"If you do it, I will make out with you." My head kept flicking back and forth, as though I were watching a tennis match. I got the impression that these people knew each other, but I wasn't in on the joke. My attention turned back to the woman behind me as she grabbed her hair with her left hand and suddenly ripped off her wig.

It was just like an episode of *Melrose Place.*

I gazed at her bald scalp, focusing on the few wisps of fine blond hair that remained. Then the room erupted in applause. She revealed that she was undergoing chemotherapy for cancer, and she'd bottled up a lot of her emotions about her illness that she'd been able to express only on her blog. "The first entry my husband ever read on my blog was the post about how bad it's been for me. He cried and asked me, 'Why did you keep this all inside of you?'" The woman was now crying too, and I felt that I should hand her a tissue. I kept a lot of things in my purse—floss, earplugs, and a one gigabyte USB drive—but I didn't have any Kleenex. It was funny that her blog had helped her deal with her illness, whereas mine had revealed how many of my readers didn't understand what I was going through at all. That might have been because my readers found my blog while looking for weight-loss help, whereas her readers were probably people who'd faced cancer themselves and knew what it was like.

The session went twenty minutes over the scheduled time and eventually broke up because the keynote was about to begin. I stood up from my chair and felt as if we should close the meeting with a big group hug. I felt a strange catharsis after all the sharing and began to understand the appeal of AA meetings or group therapy. I looked at all the occupied chairs in the room. It was sad that so few chairs sat empty, that there were so many of us to fill this room. Yet I was glad to know that these people existed, walking among me in the hallways of this hotel, looking just like everybody else, knowing what it was like to be me. There are few sounds more pleasant to hear than your own name, and there are few feelings more comforting than being with people who are like you.

On the plane trip home from the conference, I'd checked in late and been assigned a seat in the middle of the row. The flight wasn't completely full, so I had hoped the seat next to me would remain empty, but three minutes before the flight attendant closed the door, an elderly woman walked down the aisle and sat next to me. She had reading glasses hanging around her neck on a silver beaded chain. She wore a vest that looked handmade, and she carried a bag that contained part of a patchwork quilt she was sewing. I was surprised she'd gotten her pins and needles through security, when I couldn't even bring a bottle of water through the screening area.

I ignored her and focused on my book, but within twenty seconds she asked, "May I ask what you're reading?" Uh-oh. We had a talker.

"It's called *The Truth About Chronic Pain,*" I told her. "It's got lots of interviews with patients, doctors, and other experts."

"I only ask because I saw the word 'fibromyalgia' on the page there, which I have."

This piqued my interest. "I've heard of that. It causes pain in the joints and muscles, right?"

"Yes. I see the person interviewed in that book doesn't believe it's real, but trust me, it's real. I have it." I believed her. A friend of mine had also been diagnosed with the disease in high school. "I'm Mary Jane," she told me. I introduced myself, and we talked for the rest of the flight about different treatments for chronic pain. Mary Jane had tried acupuncture and chiropractic treatment, too, and was a fan of deep-breathing techniques. We talked about pills and doctors and insurance. By the end of the flight I was sad our conversation had to end, even though I had dreaded speaking to her when she'd first greeted me.

Despite these positive experiences with other people suffering from chronic illnesses, I still avoided blogging about my headache. I was happy to hear that other people had found support by writing about their illnesses, but I still got buried with advice and sympathetic comments whenever I wrote about my headache. Most of the people who read my blog did not have chronic illnesses, so they didn't quite understand how to respond to me. It was better to keep some things to myself, shared only with family and friends or a specific community.

The blog conference had renewed my interest in the online community of pain sufferers, so I spent a few days reading more stories on blogs and forums. This time I even left a comment here and there instead of lurking. I couldn't deny I was a part of this community any longer, so I might as well participate. There were people who had recently entered the world of constant misery and people who'd been living in the kingdom of the ill for years. Many of them had it worse than I did. Several of them had to visit the emergency room regularly when their migraines morphed into invisible Tasers sending shocks down their optic nerves. I read about a woman whose back pain was so intense that she'd had surgery to implant a device connected to her spine. It sent electric signals into her spinal cord that mediated the pain. Others bemoaned problems with prescription painkillers, either that they had become addicted to them or that they were afraid to use the amount that they truly needed for fear of becoming addicted. There were mothers and fathers who felt they were letting down their families because they couldn't work anymore.

I felt bad for feeling so depressed and mildly suicidal last year. What right did I have to consider killing myself when there were so many people out there who had it worse than I did? At least I was hobbling along. I wasn't able to do all that I wanted to do, but I could go through the motions. I'd been maintaining my weight for two months now and crossed my fingers that the trend would continue. The better I learned to cope with my pain, the better I seemed to cope with my urge to overeat. This was a welcome reprise from seeing the numbers on the scale inch ever upward, wanting to stop them, but still feeling endlessly compelled to suffocate the pain with a bag of marshmallows.

I turned off the computer and noticed that my desk had gotten cluttered. I started to straighten up the piles of paper and sorted through my mail, figuring out what items to file and which ones to trash. Once I'd reached the bottom of the stack, I picked up the pile of books on the carpet. I'd been reading books with titles like *Massage for Dummies* and *Heal Your Headache* and *Pain: The Science of Suffering.* I had purchased some of them, and others were checked out from the library. I filed them on my bookshelf. Since I was on a roll, I pulled the vacuum cleaner out of the closet and started sucking up cat hair and dust. Before I knew it, I was washing the dishes and scrubbing the faucet clean of water stains. It was comforting to clean. I could put my apartment in order, if not my life.

I looked at the clock on my microwave and saw that it was now eight o'clock. I had made it through one hour by cleaning. Now I would have to make it through the next hour. Eventually I would make it through the whole day. Then I'd make it through the day after that, until I made it through the week. Before I knew it, I would make it through the month, and then the month after that, until I'd made it through another year. That was how my life would go.

The clock on the microwave clicked forward a minute to display 8:01 in neon green numbers.

13

Leaving the Waiting Room

To: Jennette.Fulda@home

From: Julie@Thanks

Subject: Pain

For the last two years I've been dealing with chronic pain. And by "dealing with", I mean suffering with, figuring out how to exist with, trying to decide if life is worth continuing if I have to live in so much pain, that's what I mean by "dealing with". The thing I've found both amazing and oddly comforting in reading your blog is that—IT'S NOT JUST ME! Dear god, it's NOT JUST ME! I thought all the nosy stupid people in the world making the dumbest stupidest suggestions in the world thinking they were "helping" me were doing it because they thought "I" was too stupid!

You know the worst part about it all? I'm a chiropractor! A woman of skill and learning and science! For the past two years I've had people suggesting to me the most stupid, asinine remedies ("I've heard that moving your bed to the southwest corner of your bedroom really helps!" "Have you tried wearing rose quartz jewelry? Its vibrations really help!") I even had one friend come up to me at a picnic last summer and say "I liked you better when you were healthy." He tried to pretend he was joking, but you don't say something like that and not mean it.

So I read some of the things people write in your comment section and I realize it's not me. It's them. It's people. They're . . . people. They don't understand. I guess they just mean well? Or, they really are just that dumb. I've been in such pain that I've felt like I'm on fire, literally, and I just don't think people get what that feels like.

Anyway, thank you for your blog and your honesty and for, I don't know. Just thanks. As maybe a little ray of hope for you, about two months ago, I started to feel better. I have no idea why - I do a bunch of things to help

> me feel better. I can't tell you what if any of them made a difference and I wouldn't suggest any of them to you anyway, our situations are way different. But about two months ago, on a Friday morning, I woke up and about 90% of my pain was gone. It's not been totally perfect since then, but it's been really awesome a great deal of the time. May you have the same sweet relief tomorrow.

I knew something was wrong when I didn't feel like crap. I was in line at the grocery store, silently cursing the elderly woman in front of me who was slowly scrawling her signature on a check. I glanced over the yellow packages of M&M's at the faster line I should have picked, when I suddenly noticed it. It was the feeling I got when I went to work without my lunch bag or when I forgot to pack my cell phone charger on a trip. My head didn't hurt that much.

I could still feel the headache stomping around in my head like the uninvited squatter it was. Yet now it sounded like someone had stapled foam padding to the walls of its apartment, partially soundproofing the painful vibrations from reaching the rest of my head. Normally the stress of waiting in this endless line at the store would have been an invitation for the headache to start slamming doors and pounding on the ceiling. Instead, I felt like my normal, moderately crappy self.

How bizarre, I thought, but before I could reflect on the situation further, the conveyor belt starting jerking forward and I had to dig out my grocery rewards card for the cashier. I went home. I unloaded my groceries. I went to sleep that night.

I woke up around nine o'clock the next morning. Usually I started Sundays by crawling out of bed and making the long hike from my bedroom to the living room couch. I would then hum along to the theme song trumpeted on the CBS morning show, pretend to understand the complex discussions about war on ABC, and then flip over to PBS so I could imagine I would one day cook as well as the chefs in the test kitchen. If I was up to it, I might warm my thighs with my laptop and answer a few emails in between commercial breaks, at least until my eyes started to burn. For the rest of the day I might watch a movie or just lie on the couch staring at my stuffed monkey while I quietly berated myself for being an unproductive waste of a human being. If I was feeling particularly energetic, I might stumble down the stairs to my car and drive to the grocery store to buy a half-gallon of mint–chocolate-chip ice cream.

That was my typical Sunday. Today I didn't want to leave the house for ice cream. Instead, I was entertaining the idea of exercising. The thought bubbled on the surface of my mind unexpectedly, and I half-expected the bubble to pop before I summoned the will to get off the couch, but it didn't. *I will get up and go for a walk on the trail. Yes, I will do this. I* can *do this.* I heaved myself up from the couch to put on my sports bra and running pants. As I walked by a window, I stopped. There was rain falling outside. A flash of lightning briefly illuminated the sky. My cat rubbed against my shins and looked up at me with questioning eyes. "You know, maybe I'll just stay inside today, like you," I told him.

I opened my laptop computer and began some freelance web design work I'd taken on for a friend of a friend. *Don't push yourself too hard,* I told myself, as if I were running a half-marathon again and warning myself not to run too fast at the start so I wouldn't exhaust myself before I could finish. I'd trained myself to work for only an hour or two at a time, leaving so many words unwritten and so many web sites half-coded, for fear of antagonizing my headache. I became hypnotized by the rhythm of my tasks until I glanced at the clock in the bottom right-hand corner of my computer screen hours later. Had I really been working for three hours? The headache was still mumbling at me in the background, but not loud enough to distract me.

The thought of food did manage to distract me. I went to the kitchen and opened the fridge robotically. Then I paused, wondering what I was doing. I wasn't even hungry. I was still full from some cheese sticks I'd eaten while working. I was used to going to the kitchen to experience a brief hit of pleasure during my otherwise painful day, but I didn't need it right now. I felt . . . okay. I closed the refrigerator door and looked around my apartment. I wasn't in mind-numbing pain, and I had the whole day to myself.

What the hell was I supposed to do?

I had wanted my life back, and now I didn't know what to do with it. Normally I did whatever the headache allowed me to do, which wasn't much. Looking for a distraction, I spied the box of books in the corner that I was supposed to list on eBay for my brother. *Bleh! Too tedious.* I didn't want to waste this time doing something mundane. I glanced out the window and noticed that the rain had stopped, but I was no longer in the mood to run. It was still overcast, and the trees lining the trail would be dripping residual teardrops of rain from their leaves. I sat down to watch TV but felt guilty for doing something so mindless when I finally had the energy to do all the things that I'd wanted to do for so long.

I couldn't believe I was thinking this, but I now realized that there were good things about being chronically ill. If I hadn't replied to all my emails, it wasn't because I was lazy, it was because looking at the computer screen felt like I was jabbing toothpicks into my eyeballs. If I hadn't written a new entry for my blog, it wasn't because I would rather watch TV, it was because I could focus only on something as undemanding as television. If I hadn't run, it wasn't because I was bored with exercise, it was because I couldn't bear to increase the throbbing in my head. Now that I was momentarily feeling okay, if not completely better, I had to admit that I was acting lazy, unmotivated, and bored. "Headache" had become the new "fat," an excuse for everything that was wrong in my life.

As I fondled the remote control, a small chill ran up my back, as if I had gone outside in the cold rain after all. What if my headache was not the source of all my problems? When I had first gotten the headache, my greatest fear had been that it would never go away. Now I was confronted with the fear that the headache *would* go away and my life would still suck. What if my life had become miserable over the past year and I hadn't noticed because I blamed everything on the headache?

These thoughts were too much for me, so I predictably went back to the fridge to practice my best coping technique, overeating. Yet as I stared at the white plastic yogurt cups and diet sodas, I realized I still didn't want to eat. Compulsive overeating had always been there for me, to distract me from my problems with an intense craving for pastries and pancakes. I wanted to want it, but I just didn't. It was daunting to contemplate the fact that feeling better might not make everything better, but I still didn't feel bad enough to stuff myself. I missed the familiarity of my old enemy, binge eating, wishing it were here now to taunt me and fill me with its emptiness.

My lowered level of pain continued for the next few days, but I didn't tell anyone about it. I was afraid that mentioning it would jinx me. Strangely, I almost missed the headache. It seemed impossible to be without something that had become so much a part of me. I'd been living in pain for so long that I couldn't remember what it was like to live without it. I had become a human-pain hybrid, and now I was missing a part of myself, just as if my left arm had been lobbed off.

I wasn't entirely without the pain anyway. I was still experiencing some discomfort, but I could ignore it as I went about life, categorizing it as unimportant background noise to be ignored like the sound of a leaf blower. I still heard the sound, but I didn't pay it any mind. I spent my time thinking about other things, like what to make for dinner and the fact that I had enough energy to think about making dinner. That was the luxury of not being in pain; you didn't have to think about it all the time.

I had been keeping a headache diary at the request of the doctors at the headache clinic. When I compared my recent numbers to older ones, there was a noticeable improvement. I needed to face reality. I felt better, and I'd have to learn how to deal with it.

My pain was technically still here, but my suffering had basically disappeared. Pain and suffering were siblings, similar but not the same entity. I defined suffering as my perception of pain. The weather, my job, and my relationships all affected my mood, which affected my attitude toward the headache. Something had shifted, and now I was not suffering as I had been.

I wasn't sure what to credit for my remarkable half-cure. Were the latest pills little capsules of magic? Perhaps. I was also minding the behavioral recommendations I'd been given, such as to go to bed at the same time every night, drink less caffeine, and avoid alcohol (even though I barely drank anyway). The long Indiana winter had sputtered out, and there was sunshine so bright that I had to wear sunglasses outside. For the first time in months, my winter coat stayed in my closet when I left the house. I'd even started taking walks by the downtown canal during my lunch break in an effort to lose weight. My behavioral psychologist had been bugging me so frequently to exercise that I wondered if he moonlighted as a Weight Watchers leader.

I'd been doing more and more freelance web design in my spare time, too, which made me feel fulfilled in a way my day job had failed to recently. I was in a small team near the bottom of the hierarchy of power in my organization, so we had little control over what tasks we were assigned or how we were to complete them. This left me feeling powerless and discontented. When I went home and worked one-on-one with clients, I felt that I was helping people and making a difference in their lives. I couldn't see their faces as we emailed, but I could feel them light up when I made their sites prettier than they'd hoped for. That work mattered to me in a way my other job didn't.

I was becoming more and more certain that the day job had to go. I had already spent too much of my life experiencing pain. There was no need to voluntarily subject myself to more of it. I enjoyed bantering with my co-workers, who were smart and talented, but the negative aspects of my job were too great to ignore. Working on projects of my own made me feel energized in a way I hadn't felt since I'd written my first book. It was hard work, but it had given me a sense of purpose. Now I had something of my own again, and I just needed the guts, and the six months of living expenses in my savings account, to take the leap.

This might have been one of the few gifts the headache had unexpectedly given me. It had made me brave. People who'd had near-death experiences frequently reported that they felt a need to live their lives for today. The headache had not killed me, but the pain had made death look far more desirable than it ever should have. If I were fortunate enough to sustain this new feeling of almost-wellness, I needed to use this opportunity to do what I wanted. The pain had bossed me around for too long. I was the boss of me now, and there were going to be some changes.

"We're going to have to amputate," I instant-messaged Sarah, my work friend.

"Why? Did they diagnose you with gangrene in your brain?" she replied.

"We'll amputate my head, and I'll live as just a body," I

continued, typing vigorously. "We can put a jack-o'-lantern on top of the stump of my neck so it won't be weird."

"Of course, because why would that be weird?"

My headache was back with a vengeance, like the sequel to an action movie, harder and faster and more intense. Everything had been going so well, and now it wasn't, and there was no reason I could determine for either state of being. I had been handed my life back, only to watch it evaporate in my hands.

"I read that they used to drill holes in your head as a treatment for chronic headaches," Sarah told me.

"I read about that, too. It's called trepanation. It sounds tempting. Personally, I think the guillotine was just a last-ditch headache remedy."

"I thought you were feeling better," Sarah said.

"I thought I was feeling better, too," I replied.

"What level are you at?" My friends and family were now as well acquainted with the pain scale as I was.

"At least a three out of five. Maybe a four. It had gotten down to a one before."

"I'm sorry." I wondered how many times Sarah had typed that to me.

I felt so stupid. After a week of feeling all right, if not cured, I'd tweeted, "I'm very hesitant to say this, but the new pills might be helping a bit. I feel only 80 percent like shit lately, less shittier than normal." Passively announcing it to the Internet seemed safer than telling people face-to-face. I had long since stopped writing about my headache on my blog because I didn't want to deal with the comments, as well-intentioned as they were. I still tweeted about it because Twitter let you post only 140 characters. There wasn't much space for followers to get preachy. Now I'd have to explain to everyone that I'd been wrong.

At least this undermined the realization of one of my other fears, which was that my headache would be cured by something ridiculously simple. I'd paid more than $10,000 in medical bills trying to diagnose this disease. What I hadn't paid in cash, I had paid in pints of blood at the medical lab. My friends were starting to buy houses, but I was busy paying for my doctors' homes. I had been delighted to be feeling better, but it was sad to think a simple pill cocktail could alleviate a year of misery. I wanted it to be more complicated or difficult to treat than that. I wanted an obscure genetic disease that they would name after me once it was discovered. Otherwise, all I could do was look back at the time I had wasted that could have been saved by a messy signature on a prescription pad.

Of course, if I had immediately been put on the same pill regimen that I was on now, I probably wouldn't have been grateful at all for my brief improvement. I would have been disappointed it was not a full cure. After the last year, I was willing to do whatever the pharmaceutical industry demanded of me to get just a partial cure, even if I had to sacrifice a goat in the lobby of their corporate headquarters.

"Has anything else changed recently that might account for it?" Sarah asked.

"I don't know. It's too hard to figure out." I felt like I'd have to float for months in a sensory deprivation tank to rule out all the variables in my environment that might be causing the headache.

"I'm sorry you're in pain all the time."

"Life is pain, Highness. Anyone who says differently is selling something, like Head On."

"That's inconceivable."

One week later I was back on instant messenger with Sarah. "You know, I think I am feeling better after all."

There was a pause before the messaging program alerted me that Sarah was typing something. "Ok, that's great."

Sensing her hesitation, I replied, "I know. I don't quite trust it either."

"I hope you're getting better, really, I do."

"Yeah," I told her. "This is all rather confusing and anticlimactic. 'I'm better! No, I'm not! Wait, yes, I am!' I'd rather this disease go out with a bang instead of a whimper."

"Your life would make for a rather lame episode of *House.*"

"True," I acknowledged. "I don't think we can turn my pain on and off like a switch, though. It's more like a dimmer light." I had read that the brain didn't have a single pain center because pain was a complex sensation processed by several areas of the mind. I'd often wished that the doctors could have removed the part of my brain that processed pain. Even if they could have, it probably would have caused more harm than good. I had initially been jealous of people I'd read about who were born with a condition that inhibited their ability to feel pain. My envy evaporated when I learned that one person with this condition had left his hand on a radiator without knowing it until he smelled his flesh burning. Another woman hadn't felt the pain of a sprained ankle that she needed to rest so it could heal. She'd continued to walk on it, which caused dead tissue in her foot to develop, which then became infected and ultimately killed her. Pain was a good thing, if it was working correctly.

"Well, I'll keep my fingers crossed for you," Sarah messaged me.

"Thanks, but how will you type?" I smiled and laughed silently, happy that I felt good enough to crack a joke, even if it was a lame one.

I checked my email to read the comments left on my latest blog entry. After another week, I had gotten up the courage to write a post telling everyone I was feeling sort of better, even if I didn't have complete relief. Most of the readers responded to tell me they were glad I was feeling good, but several people asked the same question, "Did they ever figure out what was wrong?"

I sighed. I felt like a mother with a talkative toddler who kept asking *why.* Why is the sky blue? Why don't snakes have legs? Why does Jennette have a headache? There was no answer to this particular why, or if there was, we weren't going to know it anytime soon. I didn't care anymore either. I didn't need to know why I had been sick. I just wanted to enjoy feeling better. People had first used aspirin derived from willow bark centuries ago without knowing why it worked, just that it did. It wasn't until the middle of the twentieth century that scientists answered that why. I doubted anyone in pain cared as much about *why* aspirin cured their headaches as they did about the fact that it did. I had learned to let go of the questioning. It was like asking "Is there a God?" or "What is the purpose of the universe?" I wasn't going to get a definitive answer, not in this lifetime.

People wanted there to be a narrative with a tidy ending so all the loose ends could be wrapped up. When Native Americans looked at the stars, they made up tales about how those dots of lights were first lit and where the world came from. A turtle might not actually be holding up the Earth, but it made for a good story. It gave meaning where there was none. People had told me a lot of tales about my headache. It was caused by gluten. It was a sign that a saint was possessing my brain. It was caused by my wireless Internet router. All of it was true and none of it was true. It was true for the people who believed those things and it wasn't true for those who didn't. Truth didn't matter that much. A good story mattered, if it made the world easier to understand.

I still didn't have a good story to tell about why I was feeling better. It was the pills . . . maybe. The behavioral changes helped . . . probably. I'd learned how to cope . . . most of the time. For all I knew, someone might have found that voodoo doll with my name on it and pulled out the pins. Occasionally, I had received emails from other people with constant headaches. They'd googled some combination of words that had led them to my blog. They wanted help and I wanted to give it to them, but like so many of my health practitioners, I couldn't dole out relief. There did not seem to be a quick and easy cure for all headaches. Bodies were far more complicated than that. That was something that I'd first learned when I had lost weight. In those days, I might eat lots of fruits and vegetables one week and gain a pound, only to eat a tray of cinnamon rolls the next week and lose a pound. The headache seemed to be similarly nonsensical.

My weight was still a matter of concern, though the size of my thighs seemed somewhat trivial compared to my fourteen months of constant pain. I was comforted by the fact that every medical test I'd taken during that time said I was disgustingly healthy. I had benign instances of venous angioma, heart murmur, and perhaps scoliosis, but none of those conditions caused me any trouble. I may have been fatter than I used to be, but I was still fit. However, I still hated to step on the scale and see that I'd gained forty pounds from my lowest maintained weight. This was what happened when you ran to the grocery store more often than you ran on the treadmill. I sighed in disappointment, but the exhalation of breath did nothing to lessen the number on the digital display.

I had heard many women moan about their baby weight, but no one had ever complained to me about their headache weight. I hadn't packed on pounds due to a pregnancy, but I was tempted to start telling people I had so they'd be more sympathetic to my situation. I might have done it if the lie hadn't required making up an imaginary child that I would have to imaginarily raise for eighteen years. I still got emails from people who'd read my weight-loss memoir or my blog who congratulated me and told me I was an inspiration. I didn't know what to tell them. I'd mentioned my weight gain on the blog, but evidently these people had not read the "About Me" page. I wanted people to understand that my relapse was not due *just* to laziness and apathy, but that it was also the result of a medical problem that had practically destroyed me. Yet, whenever I told someone I'd had a headache for more than a year, they didn't seem to understand what that had to do with my weight. My answer? "I've been in a lot of pain, and I needed the ice cream."

When my old college roommate found me on Facebook and invited me to run a 5K race with her, I logged onto the online registration site and typed in my credit card number right away. I had learned that accountability was a key ingredient in weight loss, so now I was accountable to the Baptist Hospital in Lexington, Kentucky. Three months from now I'd have to run 3.1 miles or forfeit my free T-shirt.

I found a running plan called "Couch to 5K" which would prepare me for the race by interspersing intervals of walking and running, increasing intensity until I could run a 5K. I suited up in my running clothes and headed for the trail. The last time I'd stuck to a regular running schedule was more than a year ago when I was preparing for the half-marathon. I was proud to have finished that race, but the endeavor had burned me out. I'd been walking a lot lately, but I hadn't run for months.

The gate in the chain-link fence made its familiar clanking sound as I stepped onto the trail. I began to walk for five minutes to warm up and felt something unexpected that had nothing to do with the pain in my head. It was fear.

What if I'd forgotten how to run?

Was that even possible? The popular phrase was "like riding a bike," not "like running a race." My digital watch beeped after five minutes, and I picked up my pace. I ran for one step and then another. Then I ran a third step and a fourth, which was followed by a fifth and a sixth, and now I was running along just as I always had. After another five minutes I was panting, too, *not* like I always had. I was out of shape, but at least I still remembered the motions. If I came out to the trail day after day I would improve, and maybe I could run those 3.1 miles in three months after all.

After taking a short walking break, I started to run again. My mind wandered, falling into a state of meditation I hadn't realized I'd missed. It was easier to think out here because my body remained preoccupied, bouncing along in a soothing rhythm, while my mind was free to do as it pleased. Thump, thump, thump, thump, I plodded down the trail and was passed by a particularly fast speed walker. The headache was on the trail with me, too, but I had brushed it aside so it was only a blur in my peripheral vision. I would have preferred a complete cure, and even more than that I would have preferred a clean, simple cure with an obvious cause instead of this indefinite state. When you did the hokey pokey, you put your right foot in and then your right foot out, but I seemed to have my headache stuck over the line, neither completely in or out of pain.

I was still grateful, though. There were thousands of people in the world who would never get any relief. I also had it better than the people I'd seen at the pain seminar, the attendees at the patient blogging session, and the anonymous folks who posted on message boards every day pleading for help that was never going to come. I didn't know anything that would help those people. I would not be thumping rubber soles against asphalt right now if I still felt the way

I had on my worst days, huddled in a cocoon of cotton sheets trying to smother the pain with darkness. There was only so much a positive attitude and healthy living could do. When the pain comes for you, there is no hidden trapdoor you can climb through to escape your body.

A friend of mine from the Pacific Northwest had told me that people in Seattle panic over the smallest snow flurries. An inch or two of powder on the roads can shut down schools. It's a contrast to what I had seen on my recent trip to Colorado, where my brother and I had been part of a caravan careening through the mountains on steep, icy roads. People in Colorado put on their parkas and ski hats and drive SUVs with chains on the tires. It snows there a lot, and they can't stop that, so they've learned how to deal with it. The snow is just as cold in Colorado as it is in Seattle or in Indiana. I felt that I was finally learning to cope with the snow in my life instead of shaking my fist at the sky to curse it.

As good as I felt, I also knew I might not feel this way forever. The pills could stop working. For six years I'd been on headache medication that had worked until it didn't. There was no reason that couldn't happen again. I needed to do as much as possible with this time while it lasted, however short or long that was. There was no cure for chronic illness, just management. I would have to keep running several times a week to maintain my physical fitness. I would have to keep tending to my headache for the rest of my life to keep it locked in the partially soundproofed room I had trapped it in, praying it never broke the lock.

• • •

A small window appeared on my computer screen, alerting me that I had a new email in the inbox of my work account. I opened the program and read the latest message.

"Oh man, you've got to be kidding me," Dave moaned from his desk across the room. My eyes momentarily darted in his direction and then back to the email. It was a letter from the CEO of the company. There was going to be another furlough. I would have another week off without pay.

My boss walked into the work area and stood among the six desks occupied by his underlings. He had come straight from his office, not bothering to put down the can of Coke Zero he was sipping. "I'm sorry, everyone, but it's true. There is going to be another round of furloughs." My co-workers all slumped in their desks, looking like wilted flowers.

I clapped my hands together and exclaimed, "I'm going to Europe!" My boss choked and nearly sprayed the carpet with a shower of soda.

"Are you serious?" he asked.

"Yes! I've never been to Europe, and I've always wanted to go. I was thinking of going in September, but if I'm getting a week off in May, I'm going to do it then." I'd been reading a blog by a woman who took an international vacation every year. She traveled alone and seemed to have a fabulous time. Reading her entries had put ideas in my head that had taken root and were now blossoming. I was twenty-eight years old, and if I wanted to go to Europe, the only thing stopping me was myself.

Elliot, who sat at the desk closest to mine, grinned and nodded his head approvingly. "Where are you going to go?" he asked.

That was a good question. "Uh, I don't know," I told him honestly. I had never left the country before. I'd gotten my passport seven years ago because my family was going on a Mexican cruise. Then I'd decided to stay home to finish college summer school classes instead, so I'd missed the luxurious dinners where they folded your napkins like swans. I was determined to get some stamps in my small blue passport. It seemed that everyone I knew had traveled abroad. My older brother had lived in Venice for a semester, and my mother had traveled around the world before I was born, taking the long way home from her two-year stint as a Peace Corps volunteer in Palau. My friends had fabulous photos of themselves standing in front of the Colosseum or the Louvre. I wanted my own cheesy tourist photos, and I wanted them without Photoshop's help.

I couldn't remember a time when I didn't want to go to Europe, yet I'd never done anything about it. I'd been in debt after college, so I'd never had the money to travel. For the most part, the souring economy had been bad news because it had forced me to take unpaid furloughs and made my retirement account shrink more than my weight ever would. However, it had also driven down prices on transatlantic flights. I had calculated that a weeklong European vacation could cost less than $2,000, if I were frugal. In comparison to the price of an MRI, that was cheap, and thirty minutes inside a huge magnet was hardly as entertaining as London would be.

Every time I'd written a huge check for medical expenses, I'd told myself that it was a necessity. It was a non-negotiable expense. I decided my vacation now qualified as non-negotiable, too. I was feeling reasonably well most of the time, if not fantastic. I didn't know how long that would last. I needed to go now when I had the money and the health to enjoy it.

After some web browsing and another week watching for deals, I snatched an airfare that made me feel as though I'd mugged a travel agent. I would fly into London and take the train through the Chunnel four days later to explore Paris. I would then spend four days there, before flying out. When I announced my plans on my blog, I got the names and numbers of foreign readers who offered to have lunch with me and show me around.

Planning the trip required time I would have previously used to stare at the television, trying desperately not to think of my headache. Now I was able to focus on my planning without taking a break every ten minutes. Yet I discovered I could still rattle the headache's cage, particularly after three additional hours on the computer after an eight-hour shift at work. The headache started banging on my skull again. The monster was rattling the lock on its door. I shut down the computer and read a French guidebook instead, which didn't strain my eyes like the light from the monitor. There were several walking tours listed in the book, through historic Paris and the hills of Montmartre. Had I read that right? Hills? I thought of my recent performance on the trail. I started walking even farther during my lunch breaks. I had twenty-one days to build up enough stamina to climb the stairs of the Tower of London.

• • •

I sat in a black, vinyl chair at the airport, watching the shoes of the people walking by. Red high heels—*hope she doesn't have to run to her gate*. Hiking boots with dried dirt on top—*bet he actually used those to hike.* Bright pink Crocs—*yeah, they're ugly, but easy to take on and off at security*. I looked down at my own feet. I was wearing blue-and-white running shoes and sweat socks. *Traveler prepared to walk.*

No one was sitting in the two chairs next to me. I had placed my carry-on bag and my backpack in those empty seats. I'd managed to pack all my clothes, toiletries, and my international outlet converter into these two bags, opting not to check an item. The baggage handlers couldn't lose luggage I didn't give them. I double-checked my backpack. I had my container of naproxen, which I would take as a headache abortive if my pain started to flare up. I'd filled my water bottle at the water fountain next to the restroom after I'd gotten through security. It was important to stay hydrated. I also had two energy bars in case I needed to boost my blood-sugar levels. The doctors had told me it was important to eat every three hours or else the headache might come out to play. I had gone for a run in the morning before leaving the house because exercise seemed to lower my pain levels.

I had calculated that I would be spending twelve hours traveling. I had caught the bus from Indianapolis to Chicago and then hopped on the metro headed to the airport. Then I had hopped off the metro to hop on a shuttle bus because the metro line was under construction, which I would have known if I'd read the fine print by the asterisk on the schedule. I'd felt my neck and shoulders tense up while I worried that I'd miss my flight, but practiced my deep breathing to relax. Finally I was dropped off at a metro station three stops down the line, which I took to O'Hare, where I checked in within twenty minutes of the deadline for international flights.

I was sitting comfortably now, watching people's shoes, but soon I'd be on a plane for more than eight hours. Then I'd have to take the Tube, transfer once, and get off at the right station so I could walk through London to the hostel where I was staying. This seemed like a lot of time, but then I remembered that a hundred years ago such speedy transit did not exist. Centuries ago some people lived their whole lives within a few miles of their home. If they got headaches that didn't go away, that was just too bad. They didn't expect there to be anyone who could fix them. In some ways I was spoiled to have believed all pain should be curable. It was such a modern idea.

I was going to try to sleep on the plane, but I doubted I would be able to, which meant I was going to miss a night's sleep and go directly into the next day. The headache wouldn't like that, but until affordable teleportation was available, there was no way around it.

I checked my watch. The flight should be boarding soon. My friends who'd vacationed in Europe had told me I was going to have a great time. My mom had dropped me off at the bus stop and told me I was going to have a great time. I too hoped I would have a great time. The problem? I wasn't sure if my body was going to let me have a great time.

Despite my partial recovery, I realized this uncertainty was never going to go away. My body was a wild card. I had a chronic illness and I probably always would. There would be good days and there would be bad days. When I woke up in the morning, I wouldn't know what kind of day it would be, but I would find out soon enough. It had been that way for the past two months.

On good days, I'd made my oatmeal and savored my coffee and arrived at work on time. I'd muddled through my work, uplifted by my co-workers' jokes. I'd gone for a walk during lunch and come back refreshed, thinking, "I can do this! I can beat this thing! The headache won't get the best of me!" Then I'd eaten something healthy from my lunch bag, like a nectarine or carrots. I'd gone back to work, and by the evening I'd felt a sense of accomplishment that I'd gotten through the day. My head had started to turn up the hurt, though, because I'd sat at the computer all day. Then I'd watched some TV, and when I'd weighed in the next day, I'd thought, "I'm doing so much better. I can really lose weight now!"

On bad days, I'd made my oatmeal and burned the roof of my mouth with my coffee. I'd been thirty minutes late for work and hoped that my boss was forty-five minutes late, as he often was. I'd turned on my computer and read my emails, all from people who wanted me to do something for them, but I hadn't had the energy to put together a reply or do any of the work. I'd sighed. I'd slumped. I'd browsed the Internet for funny videos, quickly flipping back to a word-processing document if a co-worker walked by. The act of getting out of my chair to get my lunch from the refrigerator had felt like I was walking through the deep end of a pool. I'd told myself I should exercise when I got home because that would release endorphins and make me feel better, but I'd nestled into the couch instead, not because I was tired, but because being unconscious sounded so appealing.

Then I'd gone to bed and woken up the next day, which would either be a good day or a bad day. Who knew which? There was only so much I could do to control the headache. I took my pills (except when I forgot). I drove past the doughnut shop (except when I didn't). I still fought it (except when I quit).

That was how it had been and how it would probably always be. I was still visiting the headache clinic for my regular checkups. Sometimes I'd hurt so badly that I decided I would request Botox at my next appointment, no matter what the cost. Other days, I'd felt like myself again and realized how much I'd missed being the old me. I'd kept my life simple and tried not to overwhelm my body beyond its capacity to cope. I had a right to do less than humanly possible. I'd tried to keep myself occupied during the bad times, searching for anything to distract myself from the pain. I still read blogs and forums, searching for new treatments. Someday I might read about a cure for pain, but I couldn't wait forever.

There were so many things I could not control in my life, but there were other things that I could. I had decided I was going to quit my job when I returned home from this trip. I had been saving since I started the position more than a year ago, and I had six months of living expenses stuffed away. The freelance web design business I'd been doing on the side was going well enough that I was ready to go full-time. I would use COBRA for my health insurance for the maximum eighteen months. When it ran out, well, I'd worry about that then. I had looked at three-bedroom apartments with a roommate the week before my trip. We'd split the rent, and I'd have my own home office. I would be able to take sick days when I needed them without asking for permission from someone else. I knew this decision would help my health. I looked forward to my future, both the immediate part I was about to spend in Europe and the rest that would follow after that.

Sitting back in the chair, waiting for my flight number to be called, I experienced a sense of déjà vu. I didn't go to the airport that frequently except for a Thanksgiving rendezvous or a Christmas departure. Regardless, this terminal was brand new. There shouldn't be anything familiar about it. I sat for a few more seconds before I realized what it was. The airport reminded me of all the doctors' waiting rooms I'd sat in for the past year and a half, stuck between where I was and where I wanted to be. This was a waiting room, too, but for travelers, not the ill, although both places displayed signs warning me about the perils of swine flu.

I double-checked that I had my passport in my front pocket. I pulled it out to look at the picture. The photo from seven years ago had made the airport screener do a double take and ask me, "Lost a bit of weight, haven't you?"

"Yeah," I'd replied. *That's not all I've lost,* I'd thought.

Two years ago, I wouldn't have thought that. I had been a happy, healthy girl without a headache who'd lost half her weight. When I ran down the trail, I had been grateful to be part of the world, instead of sitting on the sidelines watching it pass me by. I liked that girl. She ran down a flat, even path that stretched out straight in front of her. She was unburdened. I knew what I would say to her if given the chance, because now I understood what it meant to tell someone, "You're so young."

I looked at that passport picture again. The girl who had stood at the post office seven years ago having her picture taken for this passport was even younger than the slim runner who had dashed down the trail. She had never gone to Europe. She was still fat and would get even fatter before she lost weight. She didn't have an invisible tiara of nails. She had a lot to look forward to, and a lot to dread, but she didn't know it.

I was not my old self anymore, just my new self. The name on my passport was the same, but the girl pictured there was gone, and that was okay. A picture doesn't last forever, and neither does the person in it. I rubbed the textured coating on the picture and then put the passport away.

"American Airlines flight 86 to London is now boarding rows ten through fifteen," a woman's voice sounded over the intercom. I zipped up my backpack, grabbed the handle of my rolling luggage, and boarded the plane. London was waiting for me, and I was waiting for nothing.

Resources

If you've got a headache that won't go away, or if reading about mine gave you a headache, here are some resources that might help better than chocolate and Vicodin would.

Web Sites

The National Headache Foundation—www.headaches.org

The world's largest voluntary organization for the support of headache sufferers. They maintain a list of headache specialists around the country and provide headache information and support.

Chronic Babe—www.chronicbabe.com

An online community for younger women with chronic health issues created by Jenni Prokopy. Be sure to browse the forums and sign up for the newsletter.

The Daily Headache—www.thedailyheadache.com

A blog by Kerrie Smyres that provides a candid look at managing and living with headaches and migraines.

Permanent Headache—permanentheadache.blogspot.com

Insightful blog written by another woman with a headache that won't go away.

Somebody Heal Me—somebodyhealme.dianalee.net

A blog by Diana Lee that blends news, information, and experiences about life with migraine disease, depression, chronic pain, and other chronic and invisible illnesses.

Crazy Meds—crazymeds.us

Candid information on antidepressants, anticonvulsants, antipsychotics, and other mind-altering drugs written in a funny, conversational tone by people who've taken them. Some strong language used.

MediClim—www.mediclim.com

Service that will email you a health forecast the day before your health problem may be aggravated by changes in the weather.

Clinical Trials—clinicaltrials.gov

A registry of federally and privately supported clinical trials conducted in the United States and around the world.

IHS Classification ICHD-2—www.ihs-classification.org/en

A listing of the different types of headaches recognized by the International Headache Society.

MD Junction's New Daily Persistent Headache Support Group—www.mdjunction.com/ndph

Forums for people with New Daily Persistent Headache.

WebMD: Headaches and Migraines Center—www.webmd.com/migraines-headaches

WebMD's resources for headaches and migraines.

About.com: Headaches & Migraines—headaches.about.com

A listing of information and articles about headaches.

Books

All in My Head: An Epic Quest to Cure an Unrelenting, Totally Unreasonable, and Only Slightly Enlightening Headache *by Paula Kamen*

An in-depth, darkly funny account of the author's battle with an unrelenting headache. Provides information about headache treatments and society's attitudes toward chronic pain while also recounting the author's personal story.

Life Disrupted: Getting Real About Chronic Illness in Your Twenties and Thirties *by Laurie Edwards*

Reveals forty-four tips on how to cope with chronic illness, drawn from the author's experience with a genetic respiratory disease.

Reading it is like getting advice from a smarter, more experienced big sister.

The Truth About Chronic Pain: Patients and Professionals on How to Face It, Understand It, Overcome It *by Arthur Rosenfeld*
A collection of interviews with dozens of chronic-pain experts and sufferers. Provides a broad cross-section of the different ideas and attitudes people have about chronic pain.

Pain: The Science of Suffering *by Patrick Wall*
A look at the biological mechanisms that determine how and why we experience pain, written by an expert neuroscientist. Informative, but somewhat technical.

The Pain Chronicles: Cures, Myths, Mysteries, Prayers, Diaries, Brain Scans, Healing, and the Science of Suffering *by Melanie Thernstrom*
A thoroughly researched look at pain through the filters of metaphor, religion, science, history, and the author's personal experiences. A must-read for anyone who suffers from chronic pain or knows someone who does.

Article

Here's the article I refer to in Chapter 6 about headache caused by teratoma of the ovary: Lisa Sanders, "Diagnosis: Brain Drain," *New York Times,* Nov. 7, 2008. http://www.nytimes.com/2008/11/09/magazine/09wwln-diagnosis-t.html.

Acknowledgments

Thank you to Mom, Tom, Jim (and, okay, Dad, too) for all your support, dish washing, and cooking. Thanks to my wonderful friends Cristy, Dana, and Jenny, who form a triad of awesomeness.

Thanks to Rachel Kramer Bussel for introducing me to my agent, the lovely Miss Holly Bemiss. Thank you, Holly, for all your great advice on my book proposal, and for shoving those rejection letters in a drawer I couldn't see. Thanks to Wendy McClure and Erin Shea Smith for all their advice on agents and the publishing industry.

Special thanks to Fred Choi, the editing machine, who is the master of giving great feedback without crushing my soul—in record time, too! Jen Larsen, thanks for being my book buddy! Someday our books will grow up and get married, just as we've planned, and you will receive a goat as a dowry. The ampersand in the title is dedicated to you.

Big thanks to my editor, Jennifer Heddle, for believing in this book and truly understanding what I went through. I'm glad your headache went away.

Thanks to my co-workers, especially for not moving the foosball table next to my desk. Buckets, Hats, Pancakes, Slippers, Angerballz, ZombieGuy, Dongle, and Chris—you're the best!

Thanks to my blog readers and to everyone who bought my last book. Your support has allowed me to grasp remarkable opportunities, and I am forever grateful. To everyone who emailed me with support or advice about my headache, I appreciate your goodwill. Thanks to all the doctors and healers who gave me material for this book. Special thanks to the ones who actually made me feel better. Big kisses to the manufacturers of nortriptyline, nadolol, naproxen, and all those other wonderful meds.

To find out how that European vacation went, read my travel diary at http://www.pastaqueen.com/europe.

Thank you to Jen Rios and Isabella Michon, my publicists and part-time travel agents, who worked their own asses off promoting my first book, *Half-Assed: A Weight-Loss Memoir.* Their jobs started after I turned in my manuscript, so they didn't get the credit they deserved in my last book's acknowledgments section. To my publicists for this book, I'll thank you in my next one!

A Note About Cures and Advice

You know what's wrong with me. You've got the cure and you know it for sure. You've read the book and this is something I haven't tried. You feel you must share it with me, to end my suffering, to make me well. To keep it from me would destroy you. It would make you feel like a bad person for not letting me in on the secret. Fine, if you must, you must. I cannot stop you. Email your cure to headache@pastaqueen.com and make me better if you dare.